THE AXE LAID TO THE ROOT
THE STORY OF ROBERT WEDDERBURN

Martin Hoyles

HANSIB

First published in Great Britain in 2004
Hansib Publications Limited
London: PO Box 34621, London E17 4GL
Hertfordshire: Orchard Road, Royston, Hertfordshire SG8 5HA

www.hansib-books.com

ISBN 1 870518 98 5

© Martin Hoyles

Design and production by Books of Colour, Hertfordshire

Cover design by Graphic Resolutions, Hertfordshire

For Asher and Rosa

Acknowledgements

I would like to thank the following for all their support and encouragement in writing this book: Arif Ali and Kash Ali at Hansib Publications, Shango Baku, Margaret Wedderburn Evans, Peter Garwood, Asher Hoyles, S. I. Martin, Juley Murray, Isha Persaud at Hansib Publications, David Somerset at the Museum in Docklands, Lord 'Bill' Wedderburn.

And now also the axe is laid unto the root of the trees: every tree therefore which bringeth not forth good fruit is hewn down, and cast into the fire.

Luke 3.9

Lay then the axe to the root, and teach Governments humanity. It is their sanguinary punishments which corrupt mankind. In England the punishment in certain cases is by hanging, drawing, and quartering; the heart of the sufferer is cut out and held up to the view of the populace.

Tom Paine

Let the axe
Strike at the root, the poison tree will fall.

Shelley

If you are a big tree
We are a small axe
Sharpened to cut you down
Ready to cut you down.

Bob Marley

CONTENTS

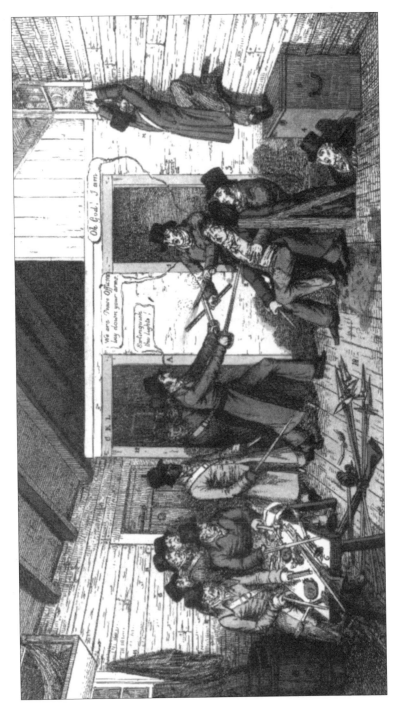

CHAPTER ONE

THE CATO STREET CONSPIRACY, 1820

Britons to arms! Stand true or be slaves for ever!

The wants of the belly create a fever of the brain.

Let us die like men and not be sold like slaves!

In London, in the spring of 1820, five men stood on trial for their lives. They had been betrayed by a Government spy called George Edwards and entrapped in Cato Street, near the Edgware Road. The charge was high treason. They were accused, with others, of plotting to assassinate the entire fourteen-strong cabinet, including the Prime Minister Lord Liverpool, the Home Secretary Lord Sidmouth, the Foreign Secretary Lord Castlereagh and the Duke of Wellington.

A contemporary chronicler, George Theodore Wilkinson, described his horror at their actions: 'It has pleased an Almighty Providence to protect the Rulers of this country from the diabolical machinations of a set of lawless wretches who sought to erect their own interest on murder, rapine and treason. Their names are transmitted to posterity, branded with the most horrible crimes that disfigure human nature; their lives are forfeited to the injured Laws of their Country: and, although they may have attempted to console themselves with the vain belief that the punishment for their deeds ends in this world, the dread reality has now flashed upon them that there is also another world in which the hardened and unrepentant sinner will meet his everlasting doom.'

But what had led these working men - shoemakers, butchers, cabinet-makers - to even contemplate such things?

One of the accused was William Davidson, a man of colour, known as 'black' Davidson. He was born in 1786 in Kingston, Jamaica. His father was the island's white Attorney-General and his mother was Black. At the age of fourteen he was sent to Edinburgh to complete his education.

Opposite: The Cato Street Conspirators

He ran away to sea several times and was twice impressed into the navy. He studied mathematics in Aberdeen for a while, but was eventually apprenticed to a cabinet-maker in Lichfield where he became extremely skilled at his job. He fell in love, was jilted and tried to poison himself. He was saved by a friend who gave him an antidote just in time.

Davidson set up in business in Birmingham, but when that failed he came to London where he taught in a Wesleyan Sunday school in Walworth. He got married to Sarah Lane, a poor widow with four sons, and later moved to Marylebone, near Lord's Cricket Ground, where his own two sons were born, John in 1816 and Duncan in 1819.

Of average height, he had dark eyes and black curly hair. He was a popular figure and invited neighbours to his birthday party where he entertained them with wine and radical songs. As a member of the Marylebone Union Reading Society, he went to meetings on Monday evenings to discuss politics and he also held similar meetings in his own house. He was an admirer of Thomas Paine, the author of *Rights of Man*.

WILLIAM DAVIDSON ADDRESSES THE COURT

On this day, 27 April 1820, in the Old Bailey the Lord Chief Justice gave Davidson an opportunity to address the jury in order to try and save his life: 'William Davidson, the law of England, in its extraordinary tenderness for persons charged with the high crime of treason, allows to the person accused an opportunity for making full defence by counsel, and you have received the great benefit the law has extended to you in this respect; but if, in addition to that which has been urged to the jury by your learned counsel, you wish to make any observation yourself, it is allowed to you to do so, and this is the proper and the only opportunity.'

Davidson was now aged 38 and stood dressed in a light brown overcoat. He spoke firmly, but politely, with a Jamaican accent: 'I am extremely obliged to your lordship for the opportunity you have given me. My Lord, from my life up, I have always maintained the character of an industrious and inoffensive man. I am a stranger in a strange land. I have no friends in England, but have always depended upon my own exertions for support. I have an extensive family, and for their sake alone is my life a value to me.

'The charge which has been brought against me, I can lay my hand upon my heart, and, in the presence of that God whom I revere, say I am not guilty of. My house has been searched and nearly pulled down and not the slightest evidence was found to show I have been guilty of any conspiracy. I was entrapped into this snare. I was not in the stable when the officers entered. They arrested me in the street. I have frequently been mistaken for other men of colour. I hope the Jury do not imagine that because I am a man of colour I am devoid of humanity.'

At this point, his throat parched, Davidson asked for a glass of water. The Lord Chief Justice agreed to his request and then replied: 'You may rest assured that your colour will not prejudice you. A man of colour is as much entitled to the protection of the law of England as the fairest man in the land. God forbid that, in the verdict of an English Jury, complexion should be taken into consideration.'

Davidson cleared his throat and continued: 'As for myself, my Lord, I have served my country, and done all that I could for it. I am a stranger to England by birth, but I was educated and brought up in England. My father was an Englishman, my grandfather a Scotchman. I may too claim the prerogative of an Englishman, from having been in the country from my infancy.'

He paused, then continued, his voice now trembling: 'Still I have not a friend in England. I have not a relative who will stretch out his hand to my helpless family. Then will you not think it hard to have my life taken away for a scene of intended iniquity, of which I know nothing. To have me torn from the bosom of her whom I lived but to cherish, to have me exposed to the ruthless knife of the executioner, while my innocent starving babes seek in vain for consolation.'

Tears strained at the back of his eyes as he turned to the jury: 'Gentlemen, when I think of this, it unmans me. I am no plotter, no assassin, no traitor. Look well to the evidence, and to your own hearts, before you pronounce the fatal verdict of "Guilty".'

Composing himself, he sighed with resignation: 'Gentlemen, I have now done. I repeat, I will readily submit to death if you think me capable of harbouring an intention to commit the crime of high treason. If that is your persuasion, pronounce your verdict accordingly. I hope my death may prove useful to my country, for still England I call thee so, and I trust that those by whom I shall be condemned, may lay down their lives with as clear a conscience.'

The Lord Chief Justice, eyebrows raised, looked sternly round the court. He pointed to the table below him on which were assembled pike handles, muskets, pistols, swords, daggers, grenades and ammunition: 'Here it is clearly in evidence that the intention of the conspirators was to murder the most respectable and virtuous characters in the kingdom. Not content with that, they were going to destroy the house of the Bishop of London, one of the most amiable men in the kingdom, who of all other men in the world is the least likely to give offence to anybody.'

He then produced a leaflet, which he held up in the air: 'I also have before me an advertisement produced by the conspirators, which you should hear. "Britons to arms! The whole country waits the signal from London to fly to arms. Haste, break open gunsmiths and other likely places to find arms. Run all constables who touch a man of us. No rise of bread, no Regent, no Castlereagh. Off with their heads! No placemen, tithes, or enclosures. No taxes, no bishops, only useless lumber! Stand true or be slaves for ever."'

With finality the Lord Chief Justice asked the gentlemen of the jury to retire and consider their verdict.

REVOLUTIONARY ENGLAND

During these years England was on the brink of revolution. The Battle of Waterloo in 1815 had marked the end of the Napoleonic Wars on the continent, but the war at home continued. The Duke of Wellington was granted £400,000 to buy a mansion and estate, but 300,000 demobbed soldiers and sailors, many of them Black, returned to compete in an already overstocked labour market. In Shropshire twenty-four out of thirty-four blast furnaces went out of production and thousands of iron-workers and colliers were thrown out of work.

The fall in the demand for manufactured goods led to a slump. Wages fell, but prices were kept artificially high, particularly after the passing of the Corn Laws which prohibited the import of cheap wheat, keeping its price at the famine level it had reached during the Napoleonic Wars.

The radical poet, Samuel Bamford, who was a weaver from Manchester, described the sudden outburst of class conflict which marked this post-war crisis: 'A series of disturbances commenced with the introduction of the Corn Bill in 1815 and continued, with short intervals, until the close of the year 1816. In London and Westminster riots ensued and were continued for several days, while the Bill was discussed; at Bridport in Dorset there were riots on account of the high price of bread; at Bideford in Devon there were similar disturbances to prevent the export of grain; at Bury St. Edmunds in Suffolk by the unemployed to destroy machinery; at Ely, not suppressed without bloodshed; at Newcastle-on-Tyne by colliers and others; at Glasgow, where blood was shed, on account of soup kitchens; at Preston, by unemployed weavers; at Nottingham by Luddites who destroyed 30 frames; at Merthyr Tydvil, on a reduction of wages; at Birmingham by the unemployed; at Walsall by the distressed;

and December 7th, 1816, at Dundee, where, owing to the high price of meal, upwards of 100 shops were plundered.'

The Government's response to all this unrest was to maintain a standing army in Britain which was larger and better armed even than the army in France, Spain or the West Indies. During the twenty-three years of the Napoleonic Wars, 155 army barracks were built in the rebellious towns and cities of Britain. In 1812 Parliament had authorized the biggest programme of barrack-building in British history. Barracks were built at Regent's Park in London for 138,000 soldiers, Liverpool for 82,000, Bristol 60,000 and Brighton 20,000. The Member of Parliament for Westminster, Sir Francis Burdett, stated: 'Ministers are intending to establish a military despotism in this country.'

At the end of 1816 huge demonstrations took place in London at Spa Fields demanding parliamentary reform, and a plot to take over the Bank and the Tower of London was uncovered. Early in 1817 the 'Gagging Bill' was hurried through parliament to restrict the right to hold public meetings, to suppress the Radical clubs and to give magistrates additional powers to prevent the publication and sale of radical pamphlets. Habeas Corpus was suspended, so people could be held in prison without trial.

Most significant of all was the meeting held at St Peter's Fields, Manchester, on 16 August 1819, when 80,000 people assembled to demand reform and the repeal of the Corn Laws. The yeomanry charged the crowd, hacking blindly with their sabres in all directions. In a few minutes eleven people were killed and over 400, including more than 100 women and girls, were wounded. Within two days the whole of England knew of Peterloo. Within a fortnight the congratulations of Lord Sidmouth, Secretary of State for the Home Department, and the thanks of the Prince Regent were communicated to the magistrates and the military 'for their prompt, decisive, and efficient measures for the preservation of the public peace'. In the weeks following the massacre there came reports of people arming and drilling all over the country.

The poet Shelley heard the news of Peterloo in Italy and wrote 'The Mask of Anarchy', although it was not published till many years later:

> As I lay asleep in Italy
> There came a voice from over the Sea,
> And with great power it forth led me
> To walk in the visions of Poesy.
>
> I met Murder on the way -
> He had a mask like Castlereagh -

Very smooth he looked, yet grim;
Seven blood-hounds followed him:

All were fat; and well they might
Be in admirable plight,
For one by one, and two by two,
He tossed them human hearts to chew
Which from his wide cloak he drew.

Next came Fraud, and he had on,
Like Eldon, an ermined gown;
His big tears, for he wept well,
Turned to mill-stones as they fell.

And the little children, who
Round his feet played to and fro,
Thinking every tear a gem,
Had their brains knocked out by them.

Clothed with the Bible, as with light,
And the shadows of the night,
Like Sidmouth, next, Hypocrisy
On a crocodile rode by.

And many more Destructions played
In this ghastly masquerade,
All disguised, even to the eyes,
Like Bishops, lawyers, peers, or spies.

Last came Anarchy: he rode
On a white horse, splashed with blood;
He was pale even to the lips,
Like Death in the Apocalypse.

And he wore a kingly crown;
And in his grasp a sceptre shone;
On his brow this mark I saw -
'I AM GOD, AND KING, AND LAW!'

Men of England, heirs of Glory,
Heroes of unwritten story,

Nurslings of one mighty Mother,
Hopes of her, and one another;

Rise like Lions after slumber
In unvanquishable number,
Shake your chains to earth like dew
Which in sleep had fallen on you -
Ye are many - they are few.

In November 1819 the 'Six Acts' were hurried through a thoroughly frightened parliament. They gave the magistrates powers to prevent meetings of more than fifty persons and to search private houses where they suspected arms were hidden. They forbade any kind of drilling or processions with bands or banners. They made publishers of 'blasphemous and seditious libels' liable to imprisonment or transportation and placed a tax of fourpence a copy on all newspapers and pamphlets. The 'Six Acts' made organized legal agitation for reform difficult and drove it once more into methods of conspiracy.

In 1820, when William Davidson stood trial, the network of barracks, which covered the country, prevented contact between the people and the soldiers, who had previously been billeted in people's houses and inns. The industrial areas in particular were treated like a conquered country in the hands of an army of occupation.

William Cobbett, the most famous radical journalist of the time, wrote of the Government: 'They sigh for a PLOT. Oh, how they sigh! They are working and slaving and fretting and stewing; they are sweating all over; they are absolutely pining and dying for a plot!' In the Cato Street Conspiracy they had their plot.

THE SENTENCE OF DEATH

On 27 April 1820, in the Old Bailey, the five men convicted of high treason in the Cato Street Conspiracy were being asked to say why they 'should not receive judgement to die, according to the law'.

The first was Arthur Thistlewood who was shabbily dressed and spoke in a mournful tone with a Lincolnshire accent: 'My Lords Castlereagh and Sidmouth will only be satisfied with revenge. They are the traitors to their country, who lord it over the lives and property of the sovereign people with barefaced impunity.

'Sidmouth has caused the murder of thousands. At Manchester my fellow-creatures were butchered without mercy. Even the innocent babe at the breast could not save the mother from destruction. High treason was committed against the people at Manchester, but justice was closed against the mutilated, the maimed, and the friends of those who were upon that occasion indiscriminately massacred. The Sovereign, by the advice of his Ministers, thanked the murderers, while yet reeking in the blood of their hapless victims!

'If one spark of honour, if one spark of patriotism, had still glimmered in the breasts of Englishmen, they would have risen to a man, for insurrection then became a public duty and the blood of the slain should have been the watchword to vengeance on their murderers. The banner of independence should have floated in the gale that brought the tidings of their wrongs and their sufferings to the metropolis.

'Such, however, was not the case, and Albion is still in the chains of slavery. I quit it without regret. I shall soon be consigned to the grave. My body will be immersed beneath the soil whereon I first drew breath. My only sorrow is that the soil should be a theatre for slaves, for cowards, for despots. Where ministers set themselves above the law, insurrection is a duty.

'I seek not pity. I demand justice. Why has the spy Edwards not been produced? Why has he not been called to give evidence? I have not had a fair trial, and, upon that ground, I protest that judgement ought not to be passed against me.'

The next to speak was James Ings who came from Portsmouth. He had become very ill in prison while awaiting trial and could hardly stand up: 'I have very little to say. My abilities will not allow me to speak. It is want of food which has brought us here.

'Death? Death would be a pleasure to me. I would sooner be hanged this instant than turned into the street there, for I should not know where to get a bit of bread for my family. And if I had fifty necks, I'd rather have them all broken, one after the other, than see my children starve.

'His Majesty's Ministers conspire together and impose laws to starve me and my family and fellow-countrymen, and if I was going to assassinate these Ministers, I do not see that it is so bad as starvation, in my opinion, my Lord. It's Edwards who has been guilty of everything. He contrived the plot, if there has been a plot. I would be very willing to die if he were to die on the same scaffold with me.'

Ings paused and then, with tears in his eyes, raised his voice: 'I don't value my life, if I cannot support my wife and children. I have a wife and four little children. I was driven to distress. I hope this man will be brought forward because I consider myself a murdered man. Edwards came to see me. I did not go to him. That man, who has got out of the halter himself by accusing others falsely, would hang his God. I would sooner die, if I had 500 lives, than be the means of hanging other men.

'There is another thing, my Lord. A meeting was called at Manchester, under the protection of the law of England, for which our forefathers died, and which King John signed in the open air. This meeting was called under the protection of that law, for the people to petition parliament to give them their rights. But, previous to the business of the meeting, the Manchester yeomanry rode in among them and cut down men, women and children in a manner that was a disgrace to the very name of Englishmen. These yeomen had their swords sharpened beforehand; and I had a sword sharpened, but I do not see any harm in that, unless the sword is used. I never used the sword I sharpened, but at Manchester they cut at women and children.

'I shall suffer, no doubt, but I hope my children will live to see justice done to their bleeding country. I would rather die like a man than live like a slave. I am sorry I have not the power to say more. I shall therefore withdraw.'

The third man to be called was John Thomas Brunt, a Welshman who spoke in a quick and hurried manner, but with a firm and confident tone. He pointed to the place above the Bench where there were texts from the Bible against false swearing: 'When I see the sword of justice and these inscriptions I feel my blood boil in my veins to think how justice is perverted and her sacred name prostituted to the basest and vilest purposes. I am a man of my word, not a shuttlecock, as some might suppose, and if I pledge myself once to destroy a tyrant, I will do it.

'I am a friend to the poor and, as an honest man, I have a fellow-feeling for my countrymen who are starving through the conduct of Ministers. The Corn Law was a blow struck against us poor devils. While they are feasting their fat guts, ours are griping. Lord Castlereagh and Lord Sidmouth have an antipathy against the people and if I conspired to murder them, is that high treason? If it had fallen to my lot to kill Lord Castlereagh or Lord Sidmouth, I would have done it and would have resisted the police-officers to the utmost of my power. But I would not have resisted the soldiers because they have sworn allegiance to their Sovereign. If resisting the Civil Power, or opposing wicked Ministers, is treason, then I am guilty. I am no traitor to my country, but I am an enemy to a boroughmongering faction which equally enslaves both the king and the people.

'I was determined when I entered into this plot that I would lose my life rather than I would betray an individual. I would be put to death, I would die on the rack, rather than I would betray a fellow-creature. This is my principle. Now Edwards was the man who always found money and who went about to old iron shops, buying pistols and swords and other things for the men who could not afford to buy them themselves. This I declare before God, whose awful tribunal I shall ere long be summoned to attend, is the truth. I have been seduced by a villain, who I have no doubt has been employed by the government.

'By hard work I used to earn three or four pounds a week as a shoemaker and while this was the case I never meddled in politics. But when I found my income reduced to ten shillings a week, I began to look about me and ask to what could that be owing. And what did I find? Why, men in power who met to deliberate how they might starve and plunder the country. Look what happened at Manchester. Nothing is too severe for men who have not only caused, but even applauded, the dreadful scenes which occurred there.

'I would willingly die as a martyr in liberty's cause for the good of my country and to be avenged on her tyrants. I joined the conspiracy for the public good. I would not have been stopped. Oh, no, I would have gone through with it to the very bottom or else have perished in the attempt.

'You may quarter my body or inflict on me every species of torture, but you will not shake my resolution or shake my spirit. I will mount the scaffold fearlessly and, if my life is called for, if my wife is to be made a widow and my child an orphan in this mighty cause, I will cheerfully sacrifice it.'

It was now the turn of Richard Tidd who, like Thistlewood, came from Lincolnshire. He was aged 45, with only a little grey hair left on his head. He was suffering particularly from the heavy weight of the irons on his hands and feet. All he said was: 'I have not had time to prepare an address, but I deny all the evidence produced against me.'

Finally William Davidson was called by the clerk. He spoke clearly but with emotion: 'My Lord, you ask me what I have to say why I should not receive judgement to die for what has been said against me? I answer that I protest against the proceedings in this trial in toto.

'In the first place, I always thought that in a court of justice the balance of justice was held with an even hand. But this has not been the case with me. I stand here helpless and friendless. I endeavoured to show that the evidence against me was contradictory and incredible, and I hoped I had made an impression on the gentlemen in the box. But the moment I was done the Attorney-General got up and told them that the evidence was pure and uncontaminated. Like a sweeping flood he bore all down before him and told the Jury to convict me.

'I do not plead for my life. I know I must fall a victim to the vengeance of my enemies. But in what manner have I been guilty of High Treason? I had no intention of joining in any scheme whatever, either to put down my King or to murder his Ministers. I was entrapped by Goldworthy and Edwards in order for some private purposes of their own that they might have my life sworn away.

'I have no objection to tender my life in the service of my country, but let me at least, for the sake of my children, save my character from the disgrace of dying a traitor. For my children only do I feel and when I think of them I am deprived of utterance. I can say no more.'

Some murmurs of sympathy from onlookers were immediately silenced by the Lord Chief Justice who rose to pronounce sentence: 'The treason of which you are charged and found guilty is that of compassing and imagining to levy war against his Majesty, for the purpose of inducing him to change his measures and Ministers, the first step toward effecting which was the assassination of ministers themselves. This is a most dreadful conspiracy. Your minds have been inflamed and your principles tainted by the perusal of those seditious and irreligious publications with which, unhappily for this country, the press has too long teemed. Before the commencement of the French Revolution the first beginnings were as contemptible as this and everybody knows the vast extent and the wide-spreading desolation by which these small beginnings were followed.

'Some of you have avowed your intention to have taken away the lives, and to have steeped your hands in the blood, of fourteen persons to many of you unknown. It is without a precedent to see Englishmen laying aside their national character and contriving and agreeing on the assassination, in cold blood, of fourteen individuals who have never offended any of them. This is a crime which hitherto has been a stranger to our country and I trust it will, after the melancholy example of the prisoners, be unknown amongst us.

'The judgement of the Court upon you is that you, and each of you, be taken from hence to the gaol from whence you came and from thence that you be drawn upon a hurdle to a place of execution and be there hanged by the neck until you be dead, and that afterwards your heads shall be severed from your bodies and your bodies be divided into four quarters, to be dispersed of as his Majesty shall think fit. And may the God of all mercy and grace have mercy upon your souls!'

THE EXECUTION AND DECAPITATION

I must die, but not like a slave,
To his tyrant in penitence bending;
I shall die like an Englishman brave,
I have liv'd so, and so be my ending.

I must die, and my doom is my pride;
The death that awaits me is welcome;
The demon's last pang is defied,
But a day of deep vengeance there shall come.

How shall my blood-shedders repent,
When the people's hot wrath is outpoured;
The freed world shall hail the event,
And the pride of its despots be lowered.

Hanging had been commonplace in London for centuries. From the twelfth century the favourite place of execution was Tyburn, near Marble Arch, and the last hanging took place there in 1783. Then it moved to Newgate and between 1811 and 1832 there were about eighty executions every year.

There had been a prison at Newgate since the twelfth century. It burnt down by accident in the Fire of London in 1666 and was burnt down intentionally in 1780 during the Gordon Riots. The aim was to release the prisoners and one of the leaders, a Black servant named John Glover, was heard to cry out to the keeper of the jail: 'Damn you, Open the Gate or we will Burn you down and have Everybody out.'

The rioting lasted several days and at the end over two hundred people were dead. Hundreds were arrested and twenty-five people were hanged. They included three Black people: John Glover, Charlotte Gardener and Ben Bowsey.

Forty years later, as dawn broke on 1 May 1820 the banging and scraping of wood, which had been going on all night, could still be heard outside Newgate jail. Five nooses could be seen silhouetted against the pale sky and next to them on the platform stood five coffins.

The platform and gallows had been built by torch light. So too had the crowd barriers and platforms for spectators. Ever since the previous evening large groups of people of all ranks and ages had been gathering to watch the proceedings, despite attempts by the police to move them on. Neighbouring gin shops and coffee houses hired out rooms with a

The Gordon Riots and the destruction of Newgate Prison

view and local roofs and attics were snapped up. Food was provided by sellers of pies, fried fish, sandwiches, fruit and ginger-beer.

By five o'clock a huge crowd had already begun to assemble and by seven o'clock the whole area in front of Newgate was so tightly packed that some people fainted from the pressure against the barriers. These were placed thirty yards away from the gallows in order to try and prevent the crowd from hearing any final speeches from the condemned men.

The authorities were so concerned at the enormous crowd and the sympathies of the people for the prisoners that a civil force of 700 men stood by to secure order and to prevent any attempt at rescuing the five men. Artillery had been drawn up and horse guards patrolled the nearby streets.

The Cato Street conspirators had been locked up in individual cells in the prison with two armed men in each cell. The day before their execution they were allowed to see their wives for an hour only. The wives were searched carefully, their shoes and stockings removed, their caps taken off and their hair let down. No other friends were allowed to visit them.

The usual solemn service for the condemned men in Newgate chapel had been cancelled for fear of being disrupted by sacrilegious comments. Four of the five prisoners were deists, not believing in organized religion, and they refused the assistance of the clergyman, Rev Cotton. The fifth, William Davidson, was a Methodist and had begged Rev Cotton to procure a Wesleyan minister named Rennett, who was also a journeyman tailor, but Whitehall had refused his request on the ground that such an illiterate person was not fit for such a thing.

It was now nearing eight o'clock, the hour of execution, and the bell of Holy Sepulchre began to toll. The executioner's assistant hurriedly spread great quantities of sawdust around the block to soak up the blood and the executioner removed the black cloth from the scaffold. The crowd's low murmuring broke into a loud roar as the condemned men appeared below the platform. There were shrieks and cries of 'Hats off!' and 'Down in front!' as people craned to see.

All five had been given oranges to eat and all, except Thistlewood, accepted a glass of wine to toast the king's health.

James Ings turned to Brunt and said: 'I hope my body will be conveyed to the king and that his Majesty or his cooks might make turtle soup of it!' Then he called out to the crowd: 'Oh! Give me death or liberty!'

The crowd's murmur again rose to a cheer and Brunt responded: 'Aye, to be sure. It is better to die free, than to live as slaves!'

Meanwhile Rev Cotton approached each of the men, his bible held high, declaiming: 'I am the resurrection and the life...' Each of them refused his prayers except Davidson who, while praying devoutly, squeezed his hand energetically.

Someone in the crowd called out: 'Think of God! Don't you believe in God?'

Brunt replied: 'I know there is a God!'

Ings added: 'Yes, to be sure and I hope he will be more merciful to us than they are here.' Then he turned to Tidd and said: 'Give us your hand. Good-bye!'

Tidd was overcome with emotion, muttering: 'My poor wife.'

Ings had to hold him up: 'Come my old cock-o'-wax, keep up your spirits; it will all be over soon.'

Tidd stumbled up the steps to the scaffold and when he reached the top he was greeted by three cheers from the crowd. He made a slight effort to join in and bowed to the people, who cheered again in expression of their admiration for him.

Davidson ascended the scaffold with a firm step and he bowed slowly to the crowd.

Ings started singing the song 'Oh give me death or liberty', then shouted out: 'I am going to find out this great secret. Good-bye Gentlemen. Here goes the remains of an unfortunate man.' He gave three cheers in a hoarse voice: 'This is going to be the last remains of James Ings. I'll turn my back on death.' He turned to face away from the coffins and started singing again.

Tidd interrupted him quickly saying: 'Don't Ings. There is no use in all this noise. We can die without making a noise.'

But Ings ignored him, shouting, 'Here I go, James Ings and let it be known that I die an enemy to all tyrants.' Turning to a person below the scaffold taking notes, he added: 'Recollect and put that down.' Then looking up at the enormous crowd he said: 'Ah ha! I see a good many of my friends are on the houses.'

At the suggestion of Thistlewood, Tidd again tried to persuade Ings to be quiet. Ings laughed and then fell silent.

Thistlewood turned again to Tidd: 'We shall soon know the last grand secret.'

Many in the crowd shouted 'God bless you, Thistlewood!'

He nodded his head in acknowledgement and said: 'I have but a few moments to live. I hope that you will report to all the world that I died a sincere friend to liberty.'

The executioner had now placed nooses around each of their necks.

It was Brunt's turn to speak out: 'What, Soldiers! What do they do here? I see nothing but a military government will do for this country, unless there are a good many such as we are. I see a good many of my friends round about.' The stiffener from his kerchief fell to the ground and he kicked it away: 'I shan't want you any more.' He then took a pinch of snuff and threw off his shoes.

The executioner was now tying the black caps round their heads and Ings addressed him in a mocking voice: 'Now, old gentleman, finish me tidily. Tie the handkerchief tighter round my eyes - tighter - that will do! Put the halter a little tighter round my neck or it will slip!' Then, swinging an old night-cap in his hand in a nonchalant manner, he turned to the clergyman: 'I hope, Mr Cotton, you will give me a good character! I am not afraid to go before God or man. I know there is a God and I hope he'll me merciful.'

The time had come and Davidson called out: 'God bless you all! Good-bye.'

The trap fell and a collective intake of breath went up from the crowd, followed by sighs and groans, by whistles and cries of 'Murder!'

Thistlewood struggled slightly. Tidd scarcely moved. Ings struggled and the executioner's assistants pulled his legs with all their might. Brunt suffered extremely and they hung on his legs until, after some moments, he was still. Davidson, after three or four heaves, became motionless.

When all were still, the bodies were cut down. Thistlewood's body was placed in one of the coffins with his head hanging over the end, the black cap removed and his neck exposed. A surgeon mounted the platform.

He had on a black mask down to his mouth, the rest of his face covered with a coloured handkerchief, his hat slouched down, wearing a blue jacket and dark-grey trousers. He severed Thistlewood's head with a knife.

The crowd booed and hissed and the masked man looked disconcerted, but handed the head to the assistant executioner who held it up by the hair, shouting: 'This is the head of Arthur Thistlewood, the traitor!'

There were groans and whistles and cries of 'murder, murder' from the crowd: 'Shoot that damned murderer! Bring out the spy, Edwards. Hang him!'

The masked man continued to decapitate the others. Tidd's head had to be held up by both hands on his cheeks because he was almost bald. The assistant executioner, however, had blood all over his hands and the head slipped out. Derisive cries of 'butterfingers' could be heard from the crowd.

When it came to Davidson's turn, the knife would not go through his neck and blood gushed out of him. Two other knives had to be used before his head was severed from his body. Several people in the crowd fainted.

The execution had lasted an hour and eight minutes. The bodies were not quartered. These were the last public decapitations in England. Susan Thistlewood, Mary Tidd, Mary Brunt, Celia Ings and Sarah Davidson petitioned Lord Sidmouth for the return of their husbands' bodies, but he refused and they were buried in quicklime in Newgate prison. George Edwards, the spy, was spirited away to Guernsey by the Government and was never heard of again.

Another Black man, Robert Wedderburn, may well have been hanged on that May Day in 1820. Along with William Davidson, he was on the Government's secret list of 33 leading reformers, but when the Cato Street loft was raided, he was already in prison, arrested for blasphemous libel. His name was Robert Wedderburn and his story begins in 1762 in Jamaica.

Opposite: The execution of the Cato Street conspirators

CHAPTER TWO

ROBERT WEDDERBURN'S CHILDHOOD

Forc'd from home and all its pleasures,
Afric's coast I left forlorn,
To increase a stranger's treasures,
O'er the raging billows borne.
Men from England bought and sold me,
Paid my price in paltry gold;
But, though slave they have enroll'd me,
Minds are never to be sold.

Still in thought as free as ever,
What are England's rights, I ask,
Me from my delights to sever,
Me to torture, me to task?
Fleecy locks and black complexion
Cannot forfeit Nature's claim;
Skins may differ, but affection
Dwells in white and black the same.

Why did all-creating Nature
Make the plant for which we toil?
Sighs must fan it, tears must water,
Sweat of ours must dress the soil.
Think, ye masters, iron-hearted,
Lolling at your jovial boards;
Think how many backs have smarted
For the sweets your cane affords.

Is there, as ye sometimes tell us,
Is there One who reigns on high?
Has he bid you buy and sell us,
Speaking from his throne the sky?
Ask him, if your knotted scourges,

Matches, blood-extorting screws,
Are the means that duty urges
Agents of his will to use?

Hark! he answers - wild tornadoes,
Strewing yonder sea with wrecks;
Wasting towns, plantations, meadows, -
Are the voice with which he speaks.
He, foreseeing what vexations
Afric's sons should undergo,
Fix'd their tyrants' habitations
Where his whirlwinds answer - no.

By our blood in Afric wasted,
Ere our necks receiv'd the chain;
By the mis'ries that we tasted,
Crossing in your barks the main;
By our suff'rings, since ye brought us
To the man-degrading mart;
All sustained by patience, taught us
Only by a broken heart;

Deem our nation brutes no longer,
Till some reason ye shall find
Worthier of regard, and stronger,
Than the colour of our kind.
Slaves of gold, whose sordid dealings
Tarnish all your boasted pow'rs,
Prove that you have human feelings,
Ere you proudly question ours!

William Cowper 'The Negro's Complaint'

Oliver Cromwell's Grand Design in the Caribbean led the English to Jamaica in 1655 after they had failed to capture Hispaniola. Previously the Spanish had occupied the island where they had wiped out the native Arawaks.

In the eighteenth century the sugar plantations grew and multiplied, along with the slave trade. Jamaican slave-holders purchased a quarter of the total British slaves in the new world. By the end of the century there were 300,000 slaves, 15 times the number of whites on the island. There

African slaves being herded to the coast

were continual slave rebellions in the Caribbean, and Jamaica experienced more than all the other British West Indian colonies put together.

Escaped slaves, known as Maroons, waged warfare against the British from the mountains. One of the most famous was Nanny who directed the guerilla forces in the Blue Mountains and was said to be able to catch cannon-balls between her buttocks and fart them back with deadly effect!

The Maroons held land in common and grew plantains, cocoa, bananas, pineapples, sweet corn and cassava; and their cattle grazed in communal pastures. Their collective spirit and common ownership were the ideals advocated by the Spenceans in England.

The colonies, however, were built on individual greed, on brutality and violence. Millions of slaves died on the way from Africa, many by committing suicide with their children. On arrival in the West Indies they were usually ill and malnourished. An English Slave-Owner's diary records: 'Captives arrive sick with dysentery. Traders plug their anuses with wadding to sell them off; flog them for not understanding English; nail their ears to trees before cutting them off; brand women's breasts; force slaves to shit in each other's mouths, piss in each other's eyes; rape and flog them; and whip anyone who says they'd rather be dead.'

By the end of the eighteenth century the economy was meant to be self-supporting. Breeding would provide a free supply of slaves. In 1788 the Jamaican Assembly passed an act entitling overseers to 20 shillings for every newborn child that survived the first two weeks of life and the same amount in tax remission to the planters. In 1792 this was increased to three pounds in order to encourage a self-sustaining source of labour, but the policy failed.

Slave women resisted, often inducing miscarriages and abortions. The self-generating workforce was sabotaged and the birthrate declined. Black women were particularly hardened against the idea of 'breeding for massa'. A slave woman, called Sabrina Park, was tried for the murder of her three-month-old child. She is quoted in the court records as having testified that 'she had worked enough for buckra already and would not be plagued to raise the child to work for white people'. According to Robert Wedderburn's father, who was a doctor, 'of those who have long been on this island, four fifths die of the venereal diseases, one way or another'.

ROBERT WEDDERBURN'S MOTHER IS RAPED, 1762

Slavery is contrary to the laws of God, Man and Nature

God made de World and de white folks made work

On the Bluecastle Estate in Jamaica, the owner James Wedderburn, from Scotland, was determined to assert his authority over his slaves. Two years earlier, a rebellion, led by a Coromantee slave named Tacky, had led to pitched battles and uprisings all over the island which lasted for months. In the end sixty white people and between three and four hundred Black slaves were killed. Two of the ringleaders were burned alive and two others were hung up in iron cages in Kingston and left to starve to death.

James Wedderburn had no doubts about what he could do with his own property and one evening spoke to his slave Rosanna in this way, 'I bought you, I own you and you shall do as I say.'

Rosanna replied vehemently, 'Le' me tell you. Me cook your food, clean your clothes, sweep your house. What more you want?'

'You know what I want and if you won't give it, then I will take it.'

'Lady Douglas would never let you suggest such a thing.'

Doctor Wedderburn became exasperated, 'You no longer belong to that old woman. God damn you! You belong to me, as do any children you may bear. I deliver babies every other day, so you'll be safe with me.'

'By Christ, you make them too! Me no want no pickney. You trick massa Douglas into selling me to Dr Cruikshank, cos you know him would never sell me to you direct. Me no carry no big belly for you.'

'Don't act so superior. I didn't pay good money for nothing.' He tried to grab her, but she sank her teeth into his hand. Wedderburn recoiled in pain.

'Don't talk dam' foolishness, man, lemme go. You been botherin' me long enough.'

'You're just like that fierce young devil Whaunica who flew at my overseer's throat at the mill and tried to strangle him.'

'What the devil you want!'

'Your hot temper and insolent behaviour will do you no good. Nor will your attempts to poison me. I know what you can do with cassava roots and why you grow arsenic beans. But you will eat first from any food you cook for me.' He moved behind her and this time managed to hold her tight, avoiding her teeth. 'Come, and afterwards you may be free.' In the moonlight he pulled her to the ground.

Years later Rosanna's son Robert imagined this moment:

To this present hour, while I think of the treatment of my mother, my blood boils in my veins; and, had I not some connections for which I was bound to live, I should long ago have taken ample revenge of my father. His mental powers were none of the brightest, which may account for his libidinous excess.

It is a common practice, as has been stated by Mr. Wilberforce in parliament, for the planters to have lewd intercourse with their female slaves; and so inhuman are many of these said planters, that many well-authenticated instances are known of their selling their slaves while pregnant, and making that a pretence to enhance their value. A father selling his offspring is no disgrace there. A planter letting out his prettiest female slaves, for purposes of lust, is by no means uncommon.

My father ranged through the whole of his household for his own lewd purposes; for they being his personal property, cost nothing extra; and if any one proved with child - why, it was an acquisition which might one day fetch something in the market, like a horse or pig in Smithfield. In short, amongst his own slaves my father was a perfect parish bull; and his pleasure was the greater, because, at the same time, he increased his profits.

My mother was forced to submit to him, being his slave, though he knew she disliked him. She knew that he was mean, and, when gratified, would not give her her freedom. I have seen my poor mother stretched on the ground, tied hands and feet, and flogged in the most indecent manner, though pregnant at the same time, her fault being the not acquainting her mistress that her master had given her leave to go to see her mother in town. So great was the anger of this Christian slave-dealer that he went fifteen miles to punish her while on the visit.

My mother bore my father two children, one of whom, my brother James, a millwright, I believe is still living in Jamaica, upon the estate.

Soon after this, my father introduced a new concubine into his seraglio, one Esther Trotter, a free tawny, whom he placed over my mother, and to whom he gave the direction of his affairs.

My brother Colville asserts that my mother was of a violent and rebellious temper. I will leave you now to judge for yourselves, whether she had not some reason for her conduct. Hath not a slave feelings? If you starve them, will they not die? If you wrong them, will they not revenge? Insulted on the one hand, and degraded on the other, was it likely that my poor mother could practise the Christian virtue of humility, when her Christian master provoked her to wrath?

Shortly afterwards she became pregnant again; and I have not the least doubt but that from her rebellious and violent temper during that period, I have inherited the same disposition - the same desire to see justice overtake the oppressors of my countrymen - and the same determination to lose no stone unturned, to accomplish so desirable an object.

My mother's state was so unpleasant, that my father at last consented to sell her back to Lady Douglas; but not till the animosity in my father's house had grown to such an extent, that my uncle, Sir John Wedderburn, my father's elder brother, had given my mother an asylum in his house, against the brutal treatment of my father. At the time of the sale, my mother was five months gone in pregnancy; and one of the stipulations of the bargain was, that the child which she then bore should be free from the moment of its birth.

I was that child. When about four months old, the ill-treatment my mother had experienced had such an effect upon her, that I was obliged to be weaned, to save her life. Lady Douglas, at my admission into the Christian church, stood my godmother, and, as long as she lived, never deserted me. She died when I was about four years old. Then my mother was sold again and I was delivered over to the care of my grandmother who lived at Kingston. I never saw my mother again.

ROBERT WEDDERBURN'S GRANDMOTHER IS FLOGGED, 1773

The crow wish'd every thing was black,
The owl that every thing was white.

Robert remembered his grandmother well:

My grandmother earned her livelihood by retailing all sorts of goods, hard or soft, smuggled or not, for the merchants of Kingston. She was the property of one Joseph Payne, at the east end of Kingston; and her place was to sell his property - cheese, checks, chintz, milk, gingerbread, etc; in doing which she trafficked on her own account with the goods of other merchants, having an agency of half-a-crown in the pound allowed her for her trouble.

No woman was perhaps better known in Kingston than my grandmother, by the name of 'Talkee Amy', signifying a chattering old woman. Though a slave, such was the confidence the merchants of Kingston had in her honesty, that she could be trusted to any amount; in fact, she was the regular agent for selling smuggled goods.

One day I went with my grandmother to see my father, for the one and only time in Jamaica, to know if he meant to do anything for me, his son. When he gave her some abusive language, my grandmother called him a mean Scotch rascal, thus to desert his own flesh and blood; and declared, that as she had kept me hitherto, so she would yet, without his paltry assistance.

This was the parental treatment I experienced from a Scotch West-India planter and slave-dealer. I was now eleven years old.

Amy was standing in the yard smoking her short pipe. She was seventy years old, dressed in a short cloak and red petticoat, with a strip of calico about her head. Round her neck she wore a string of scarlet palm-berries and hanging from her belt a string of alligator's teeth, parrots' beaks and some feathers.

With some helpers she formed a circle and in the middle stood a young man looking at her nervously. She was engaged in an obeah ceremony. Some of her assistants played a musical accompaniment on drums and flutes and a fiddle, while others were beating boards with sticks and shaking calabashes filled with pebbles.

Amy placed some cats' ears, chickens' feet, human hair, eggshells and fish bones round the man and started dancing. As she circled her victim, she sprinkled powder and blew on him. Her assistants then began to whirl him round until he lost consciousness and fell to the ground like a corpse. Amy went up to him and squeezed some herb juice into his mouth and anointed his eyes and the tips of his fingers, meanwhile chanting and howling. The corpse gradually returned to life and knelt in penitent pose. Everyone laughed and the young man staggered off, followed by the musicians.

Amy sat down and puffed on her pipe. All of a sudden her grandson Robert rushed into the yard, chased by a bigger boy. Amy stood up, arms akimbo and exclaimed, 'God Almighty! What me eye a see? If you give him licks, you'll be sorry.'

The boy stopped dead in his tracks and then retreated sheepishly, leaving behind a tearful Robert.

'Now stop you' bawlin' and hollerin' and make we hear.'

Robert made a vain attempt to hide a chicken leg behind his back and snivelled, 'I did him nothing, granny.'

'Bring come, Robert, a wha' me tell you 'bout teefin'? You' fader white, but no need you act like him. It's the English, dem steal. Dem steal us all from Africa. You' uncle and auntie been took twice. God preserve 'em. They now in America, where dem trow all the tea in the sea.'

'A fun me a make.'

'Sit here, Robert. You listen to me. You' mudder African, like me, and her still got African spirit, like Abena, Queen of Kingston. When Dr Campbell bought you' mudder, she tried to starve herself to death. Went six days with no food, to mek him sell her again. That's why you' fader couldn't keep her. You know what white folks calls you?'

'No, granny.'

'They calls you mulatto or half-caste, cos you mixed. But that's all buckras' nonsense. All you pickneys are African. One time, if you become a sailor an' go a Englan', remember one ting. You baptised in the English Church, but you' spirit African.'

Amy sighed and put Robert on her knee, 'A wha' me a go do? Me tired. Three score years and ten, a so dem say, is our time on earth, but my time's not up yet. There's higglerin' still to do.'

Robert started whistling, but his grandmother whispered in his ear, 'Remember, don't whistle in the night, or..' and they both recited together, 'the duppies will catch your voice.' They both laughed loudly.

'Granny, tell me another Anancy story.'

Amy thought for a moment and then began, 'All right. Dis one 'bout a Blackbird and Woss-Woss.' She buzzed like a wasp.

One day there was a place where they usual to kill plenty of meat. An' Mr Blackbird has a certain tree, hidin' himself. An' every cow dem kill, Mr Blackbird see how dem kill it. An' going into the house, the house don't lock with no key nor either open with no key. When they want to go in dem use a word, say 'one - two - tree - me no touch liver', an' the door open himself. An' when dem want to come out of the house dem use the same words 'one - two - tree - me no touch liver'. An' Mr Blackbird tief dem fe true, an' dem never find it out.

An' one day Mr Blackbird write his friend Mr Anancy to take a walk wid him, an' him will show him where he is gettin' all these meat. An' when he is goin' him tell Mr Anancy all the rule, that when he go on the tree he must listen, an' him will hear what dem say to open the door both goin' in an' comin' out.

What Mr Anancy did: when he see the butcher dem passin' with the meat, Anancy was tremblin' an' saying, 'Look a meat, - Look a meat.'

'Bro'er Anancy, hush you' mout', you a go mek dem shot me.'

When the butcher dem gone, Mr Blackbird come down, he an' Mr Anancy, an' go inside the house the very same as the butcher dem do, say 'one - two - tree - me no touch liver'. As they go into the house Blackbird tell him that him mustn't tek no liver. An' Mr Anancy took liver an' put in his bag. An' when Blackbird started out with the same word Mr Anancy left inside was tying his bag.

Now Mr Anancy ready fe come out of the house, count 'one - two – tree - me no touch liver', and dis time he has the liver in his bag.

The door won't open.

Blackbird call him, 'Come on!'

He say, 'The door won't open.'

Then he count more than what he was to, by get so frighten. He say, 'One - two -tree - four - five - six - seven - eight - nine - ten - me no touch liver.'

The door won't open.

Mr Blackbird say, 'Look in you' bag, you must have liver.'

The fellow so sweet-mout' say in a cross way, 'No.'

Blackbird leave him.

When Blackbird go home he look an' can't see Mr Anancy, so him fly a bush an' get up a whole regiment of soldier. Who these soldier was, was Woss-Woss. Mr Blackbird was the General, march before. When dem reach to the place they were just in time, for the butcher were taking Mr Anancy to go an' tie him on a tree to cut him with hot iron. Word of command was given from Mr Blackbird, an' by the time the butcher dem come to the door with Mr Anancy the whole world of Woss-Woss come down on dem.

They have to let go Mr Anancy. Not one of the butcher could see. Mr Blackbird soldier gain the battle an' get 'way Mr Anancy. They tek all the butcher meat an' carry home. Then Mr Blackbird tek Mr Anancy under his wing an' all his soldiers an' fly to his own country. From that day Woss-Woss is a great fighter until now, so bird never do without them to guard their nest.

Robert clapped his hands and joined his grandmother in the last line, 'Jack Mantora me no choose any.'

They both laughed again and Amy said, 'You're my yitty blackbird. But remember how him need the help of Woss-Woss to rescue Anancy.'

She took Robert off her lap and stretched her arms to the sky, 'Hungry kill me. Mek we go. Me mek some fee-fee.'

But at that moment her owner, Joseph Payne, strode on to the scene, accompanied by a male slave carrying a rope and another called Mary, who pointed to Amy, crying, 'There she is. Me saw her bewitch you' uncle's ship, before him leave. She vex cos him no free her. Keep cussing bad word.'

Amy looked at her fiercely, but said nothing.

Joseph hissed to the male slave, 'Tie up the witch!'

He bound her hands tightly above her head, threw the rope over a branch of a tree and pulled on it till her feet were nearly off the ground.

Standing on tip-toe, Amy looked firmly at Joseph and said deliberately, 'Me raise you from when you eight years old an' you do this to me.'

Joseph ignored her, ripped her dress from her back and shouted, 'You witch, damned witch! You killed my uncle with your sorcery.' He flogged her until she nearly died. Amy did not utter a sound. Meanwhile Robert had scurried under the verandah of the house and was watching like a terrified rabbit.

After he had finished, Joseph said, 'Mary, see to her.'

They released the rope and Amy dropped to the ground. Robert came up to her crying and his grandmother half moaned and half whispered, 'Woss-Woss, Woss-Woss.'

Robert stuttered, 'Come go, granny. Come go.' The two slaves carried her into the house.

In later years Robert Wedderburn remembered the consequences:

Soon after this incident my grandmother had full satisfaction. The words of our blessed Lord and Saviour Jesus Christ were fulfilled in this instance: 'Do good to them that despitefully use you, and in so doing you shall heap coals of fire upon their heads.'

This woman, Mary, had an only child, which died soon after this affair took place, plainly a judgement of God; and the mother was forced to come and beg pardon of my grandmother for the injury she had done her, and solicit my grandmother to assist her in the burial of her child.

My grandmother replied, 'I can forgive you, but I can never forget the flogging'; and the good old woman instantly set about assisting her in her child's funeral, it being as great an object to have a decent burial with the blacks in Jamaica, as with the lower classes in Ireland.

This same woman, who had so wickedly calumniated my grandmother, afterwards made public confession of her guilt in the market-place at Kingston, on purpose to ease her guilty conscience, and to make atonement for the injury she had done.

Flagellation of a female slave

As my grandmother foresaw, I did not stay long in Kingston, there being no employment. I wanted to go to sea, so at sixteen I joined the navy, and in 1779 landed in England.

The first thing I remember was seeing the remains of a rebel's skull affixed over Temple Bar. It could well have been my grandfather's. He was a staunch Jacobite and exerted himself strenuously in the cause of the Pretender in the rebellion of the year 1745. For his aiding to restore the exiled family to the throne of England, he was tried, condemned, and executed. He was hung by the neck till he was dead; his head was then cut off and his body was divided into four quarters.

CHAPTER THREE

WEDDERBURN BECOMES A METHODIST, 1785

We will be slaves no more,
Since Christ has made us free,
Has nailed our tyrants to the cross,
And bought our liberty.

When Wedderburn came to Britain in 1779, there were already between 10,000 and 20,000 Black people living in the country. (This compares with a police estimate of 25,000 in 1953, when the population of the country was over five times greater.) Many were escaped slaves and servants and many had just arrived after the British defeat in the American War of Independence. In London they congregated in the slums of Paddington, Whitechapel and St Giles-in-the-Fields, alongside Jewish and Irish immigrants. Life was rough, but they survived and were known as blackbirds.

Wedderburn knew, however, that there should be a better way of life:

For seven years I lived amongst a set of abandoned reprobates, conscience frequently smiting me and telling me that the way I was pursuing was the road to everlasting ruin. To lull and calm these reflections, I frequently promised to reform, but Sin being such a constant companion, and so sweet to my taste, my efforts and strivings were in vain.

Passing Seven Dials one Lord's day, I stopped to listen to a preacher of Mr. Wesley's connection.

Seven Dials was in the parish of St Giles-in-the-Fields, known as the Rookeries. It consisted of the worst living conditions in the whole of London's history and had the second highest mortality rate in the entire city. A small group of landlords made money out of the wretched accommodation of the people who lived in the area. Over fifty people of both sexes could be living in the same house. Broken windows were stuffed with paper and the floors and walls were damp. The narrow streets were filthy and the stench indescribable. The place was overrun with vermin, and diseases, such as cholera, were rife.

The population consisted of labourers and beggars, prostitutes and tramps, discharged soldiers and sailors, thieves, road-sweepers, knife-grinders and street-singers, makers of doormats, shoemakers and street-sellers. In one small place could be found twenty people selling their wares: oranges, onions, herrings, watercress, shrimps, pincushions, birds, prints and ballads, medicines, pills and potions.

It was the kind of place a Methodist preacher would go to save souls. In fact, earlier in the century, John Wesley had set up a meeting house in the area. The Church of England was not concerned with the urban poor, but the founder of Methodism was determined to bring the gospel to the down and out. He toured the country preaching to the working classes in mining districts and manufacturing towns. Far from being a radical, however, Wesley was a high Tory in politics: 'The greater the share the people have in government, the less liberty, civil or religious, does a nation enjoy.'

John Wesley

But he was opposed to slavery and expressed his views in a book published in 1774 entitled *Thoughts on Slavery*. In 1791, the last year of his life, he read Olaudah Equiano's slave autobiography, which had been published a couple of years earlier, and the last letter he ever wrote was to Wilberforce expressing his view that slavery was 'an execrable villainy which is the scandal of England and of human nature'.

Many early Methodists were more radical than Wesley, however, and Tom Paine, for example, the most famous eighteenth-century radical and the author of *Rights of Man*, was once a Methodist lay-preacher. Unlike Calvinists, who held the view that only a preordained elect could be saved, Methodists believed that salvation was available to all. Rich and poor alike could be saved from their sins and were equal in the sight of God. This is what appalled people like the Duchess of Buckingham who hated Methodists: 'Their doctrines are most repulsive towards their Superiors, in perpetually endeavouring to level all ranks and to do away with all distinctions. It is monstrous to be told you have a heart as sinful as the common wretches that crawl on the earth.'

Amongst these 'common wretches' in Seven Dials, Robert Wedderburn stopped to listen to the preacher, who by then was in full flow. He stood on an upturned vegetable crate next to some helpers with tambourines, and already there was a large crowd gathered to hear him, several of them Black. His voice rose loud and clear above the city sounds and the barking of dogs. At various points the audience responded in support or raised drunken cheers:

I would to God that we may never more steal and sell our brethren like beasts, never more murder them by thousands and tens of thousands. O may this worse than Mahometan, worse than pagan abomination, be removed from us for ever! Never was anything such a reproach to England since it was a nation, as the having any hand in this execrable traffic.

The slave-holders say they are authorized by law, but can law, human law, change the nature of things? Can it turn darkness into light, or evil into good? By no means. Notwithstanding ten thousand laws, right is right and wrong is wrong still. There must remain a difference between justice and injustice, cruelty and mercy. So that I still ask: Who can reconcile this treatment of the negroes, first and last, with either mercy or justice?

Where is the justice of inflicting the severest evils on those that have done us no wrong? Of depriving those that never injured us in word or deed, of every comfort of life? Of tearing them from their native country and depriving them of liberty itself? An Angolan has the same natural right as an Englishman to liberty, on which he sets as high a value. Yea where is the justice of taking away the lives of innocent, inoffensive men? Murdering thousands of them in their own land by the hands of their own countrymen; many thousands, year after year, on shipboard, and then casting them like dung into the sea!

'However this be', say the slave-holders, 'it is necessary when we have slaves to use them with severity.' What, to whip them for every petty offence till they are all in gore blood? To take that opportunity of rubbing pepper and salt into their raw flesh? To drop burning sealing-wax upon their skin? To castrate them? To cut off half their foot with an axe? To hang them on gibbets that they may die by inches, with heat and hunger and thirst? To pin them down to the ground and then burn them by degrees, from the feet to the head? To roast them alive?

When did a Turk or a heathen find it necessary to use a fellow-creature thus? Did the Creator intend that the noblest creatures in the visible world should live such a life as this! O Earth, O Sea, cover not thou their blood! What wonder if they should cut their masters' throats? And if they did, who could blame them?

Do these planters feel no relenting? If they do not, they must go on till the measure of their iniquities is full. Then will the Great God deal with them, as they have dealt with their slaves. And at that day it shall be more tolerable for Sodom and Gomorrah than for them!

God grant, for the honour of our country and religion, that these planters in our West Indian islands may never more be able to carry on their barbarous trade! The total, final destruction of this horrid trade would rejoice every lover of mankind, even if all our sugar-islands, as long as the inhabitants escaped, were swallowed up in the depth of the sea.

Certain it is that England may not only subsist, but abundantly prosper without them, though we no more suck blood and devour the flesh of the less barbarous Africans. O earth, hide not thou their blood and no more cover the slain! O burst thou all their chains in sunder, more especially the chains of their sins! Thou, O Saviour of all, make them free that they may be free indeed.

How does our land mourn under the overflowings of ungodliness? What villainies of every kind are committed day by day! Yea, too often with impunity, by those who sin with a high hand and glory in shame. Who can reckon up the oaths, curses, profaneness and blasphemies; the lyings, slanderings, evil speaking, the Sabbath-breaking, gluttony, drunkenness, revenge, whoredoms, adulteries and various uncleanness;

the frauds, injustice, oppression and extortion which overspread our land as a flood? Satan and sin are always near.

'He that believeth shall be saved; he that believeth not shall be damned.' Let us consider the eternal punishment of damned souls. Who can conceive their misery and torment? Who can dwell with everlasting fire?

> There thou shalt die the second death,
> And gnaw thy tongue, and gnash thy teeth,
> And welter in that fire.

Everlasting fire. If you would be everlasting happy and escape the vengeance of eternal fire or, to mention what may perhaps have more weight with some of you, if you would preserve yourselves, your families, your posterity from poverty, from slavery, ignorance, idolatry, torture and death; if you would save yourselves and them from all the infernal horrors of popery and the savage tyranny of French conquerors; in short, if you would avoid all that is terrible and enjoy everything that is dear and valuable, REPENT and turn to the Lord.

This is the only cure for our wounded country and if you refuse to administer it in time, prepare to perish in its ruins. If you go on impenitent in sin, you may expect not only to be damned for ever, but, what is more terrible to some of you, to fall into the most extreme outward distress. You will have reason to fear not only the loss of heaven, which some of you perhaps think little of, but the loss of all that lies so near your hearts.

And will you not repent when you are pressed to it from so many quarters at once?

> JESUS, Lord, to thee I look,
> Crush'd by my oppressor's yoke;
> From this grievous slavery
> Thou alone canst set me free.

'By grace ye are saved, through faith.' Ephesians chapter 2, verse 8. If thou shalt confess with thy mouth the Lord Jesus, and shalt believe with thy heart that God hath raised him from the dead, thou shalt be saved. 'Whosoever believeth on him shall be saved' is and must be the foundation of all our preaching.

'Well, but not to all.' To whom then are we not to preach it? Whom shall we except? The poor? Nay, they have a peculiar right to have the gospel preached unto them. The unlearn'd? No. God hath revealed these *things unto the unlearn'd and ignorant men from the beginning. The young? By no means. Suffer these in any wise to come unto Christ and forbid them not. The sinners? Least of all. He came not to call the righteous, but sinners to repentance. Why then, if any, we are to except the rich, the learned, the reputable, the moral men. And 'tis true, they too often except themselves from hearing, yet we must speak the words of our Lord. For thus the tenor of our commission runs. Go and preach the gospel to every creature.*

Here is comfort, high as heaven, stronger than death! What! Mercy for all? For Zaccheus, a public robber? For Mary Magdalene, a common harlot? Methinks I hear one say, then I, even I, may hope for mercy. And so thou may'st, thou afflicted one, whom none hath comforted. God will not cast out thy prayer.

> *Look, and be sav'd from sin;*
> *Believe, and be ye clean!*
> *Guilty, lab'ring souls, draw nigh,*
> *See the fountain opens wide,*
> *To the wounds of JESUS fly,*
> *Bathe ye in my bleeding side.*

Go forth then, thou little child, that believeth in him, and his right hand shall teach thee terrible things. Though thou art helpless and weak as an infant of days, the strong man shall not be able to stand against thee. Thou shalt prevail over him and subdue him, and overthrow him, and trample him under thy feet. Thou shalt march on under the great captain of thy salvation, conquering and to conquer, until all thine enemies are destroyed, and death is swallowed up in victory. Praise the Lord! Hallelujah! Hallelujah!

> *Come sinners, to the gospel feast;*
> *Let every soul be Jesu's guest;*
> *Ye need not one be left behind;*
> *For God hath bidden all mankind.*
> *Come all ye souls by sin oppresst,*
> *Ye restless wanderers after rest;*
> *Ye poor, and maim'd, and halt, and blind,*
> *In Christ a hearty welcome find.*

Let us conclude by singing Charles Wesley's glorious hymn which celebrates the mercy and forgiveness of our Lord:

And can it be that I should gain
An interest in the Saviour's blood?
Died He for me, who caused his pain?
For me, who Him to death pursued?
Amazing Love! how can it be
That Thou, my God, shouldst die for me!

He left His Father's throne above -
So free, so infinite His grace -
Emptied Himself of all but love,
And bled for Adam's helpless race.
'Tis mercy all, immense and free;
For, O my God, it found out me!

Long my imprisoned spirit lay
Fast bound in sin and nature's night;
Thine eye diffused a quickening ray -
I woke, the dungeon flamed with light;
My chains fell off, my heart was free,
I rose, went forth, and followed Thee.

Trumpets and tambourines accompanied the hymn to the tune of Sagina. During the singing a woman, dressed in rags, started acting as though possessed. She began writhing around, turning with a sort of convulsive motion in every part of her body, sighing and groaning, then whining and howling, and, as the crowd parted a little, she fell to the ground in a swoon. The preacher went up to her, revived her gradually and brought her to his makeshift pulpit, meanwhile declaiming loudly:

Blow ye the trumpet, blow,
The gladly solemn sound,
Let all the nations know,
To earth's remotest bound;
The year of jubilee is come;
Return, ye ransom'd sinners home.

He held up his arms to the sky and said, 'We praise Thee O God. We acknowledge Thee to be the Lord!' Then turning to the woman he pronounced, 'Your sins have been forgiven. 'Tis mercy all, immense and free. Go and sin no more.'

As the tambourines rattled, the woman responded, 'Glory! Glory! I the chief of sinners am, but Jesus died for me. Hallelujah! Hallelujah! Praise the Lord! I am saved!'

The preacher addressed the crowd again:

> *O all that pass by, to Jesus draw near,*
> *He utters a cry; ye sinners give ear!*
> *From hell to retrieve you He spreads out his hands;*
> *Now, now to receive you, He graciously stands.*

Then he turned to Wedderburn, who had stood mesmerized throughout the sermon, and said, 'Come, sinner, to the Saviour fly. Approach the eternal throne. The blood of Christ is sufficient. All who are willing to repent will be pardoned. Do you repent of all your sins?'

Wedderburn whispered in a scarcely audible voice, 'I do. I am a great sinner.'

The preacher placed a hand on his head, 'Your soul is cleansed by the blood of the Lamb. Your faith has made you whole.' The music started up again and they sang the last verse of the hymn:

> *No condemnation now I dread;*
> *Jesus, and all in Him, is mine!*
> *Alive in Him, my living Head,*
> *And clothed in righteousness divine,*
> *Bold I approach the eternal throne,*
> *And claim the crown, through Christ, my own.*

The preacher gave a final blessing, 'Now thanks be to God which giveth victory through our Lord Jesus Christ, to whom with the Father and the Holy Ghost, be blessing and glory, and wisdom, and thanksgiving, and honour, and power, and might, for ever and ever. Amen.'

CHAPTER FOUR

WEDDERBURN BECOMES A SPENCEAN, 1813

The produce of the land belongs to those who cultivate it

The profit of the earth is for all

Methodism had a revolutionary democratic potential, but John Wesley saw it as a means of reviving the Church of England and maintaining loyalty to the king. It was only after Wesley's death in 1791 that Methodism broke with the Anglican church. At that time there were about 80,000 people in the Methodist societies. In 1797 Alexander Kilham led a breakaway group called the Methodist New Connexion which argued for a more democratic structure and political reform. They were known as Tom Paine Methodists.

By the nineteenth century, official Methodism was striving to be more respectable and distanced itself from radical politics. Wedderburn was later to oppose their preaching of passive obedience to slaves on the plantations. He also began to be less concerned with the after-life and more determined to do something about this life.

After examining the scriptures carefully for himself, Wedderburn eventually became a Unitarian and was licensed as a dissenting minister. Unitarians did not believe in the Trinity and, like Muslims, saw Jesus as an enlightened teacher. They also rejected the doctrine of eternal damnation and torment.

The land is the people's farm

Let tyrants tremble at the crow of liberty

The years between Wedderburn becoming a Methodist and becoming a Spencean contain some of the most momentous events in history, which may help explain his move from religion to politics.

In 1789 the French Revolution began with the storming of the Bastille. Two years later a slave rebellion took place in San Domingo, the French

West Indian colony which supplied two-third of France's overseas trade and was the biggest individual market for the European slave-trade. It was the greatest colony in the world, resting on the labour of half a million slaves.

In *The Black Jacobins* the Trinidadian historian C.L.R. James describes what happened: 'The struggle lasted for 12 years. The slaves defeated in turn the local whites and the soldiers of the French monarchy, a Spanish invasion, a British expedition of some 60,000 men, and a French expedition of similar size under Bonaparte's brother-in-law. The defeat of Bonaparte's expedition in 1803 resulted in the establishment of the Negro state of Haiti which has lasted to this day. The revolt is the only successful slave revolt in history, and the odds it had to overcome is evidence of the magnitude of the interests that were involved. The transformation of slaves, trembling in hundreds before a single white man, into a people able to organise themselves and defeat the most powerful European nations of their day, is one of the great epics of revolutionary struggle and achievement.'

The leader of the San Domingo revolution was Toussaint L'Ouverture, but in 1802 he was tricked by the French, arrested and imprisoned in France where he died of cold and starvation 3,000 feet up in the Jura Mountains. The *Annual Register* of 1802 voted Toussaint man of the year and the poet Samuel Coleridge wrote of his 'true dignity of character'. On 9 November Wordsworth's poem 'To Toussaint L'Ouverture' was published in the *Morning Post*:

> *Though fallen thyself, never to rise again,*
> *Live and take comfort. Thou hast left behind*
> *Powers that will work for thee; air, earth, and skies;*
> *There's not a breathing of the common wind*
> *That will forget thee; thou hast great allies;*
> *Thy friends are exultations, agonies,*
> *And love, and man's unconquerable mind.*

Another of Toussaint's allies was Robert Wedderburn who in 1813 became a Spencean. It was the year in which Shelley's *Queen Mab* was published:

> *Let the axe*
> *Strike at the root, the poison-tree will fall.*

In January of that year fourteen Luddite leaders were hanged at York Castle. The Luddite uprising started in Nottinghamshire and

Leicestershire, but quickly spread through Yorkshire and Lancashire. It was sparked off by the lowering of wages and mass unemployment caused by the introduction of new machinery for making stockings and other clothes. Organised groups of Luddites, named after the mythical General Ludd, would visit employers who had machines in their houses and shops, smash the machines and vanish. They went on to collect arms and drill, and to organize food riots with the intention of lowering food prices.

The year before, on 27 February 1812, when he was twenty-four, the poet Lord Byron made his maiden speech in the House of Lords on a bill providing the death penalty for Luddites. 'You call these men a mob, desperate, dangerous and ignorant,' he said, but then he reminded his peers that this is the same 'mob that labour in your fields and serve in your houses, - that man your navy, and recruit your army, - that have enabled you to defy the world, and can also defy you when neglect and calamity have driven them to despair.'

The first seven Luddites to be brought to execution in York, in the presence of great crowds, came to the scaffold singing the Methodist hymn:

> *Behold the Saviour of Mankind,*
> *Nail'd to the shameful tree;*
> *How vast the love that him inclin'd*
> *To bleed and die for me.*

Also in that same year there was an epidemic of Spencean graffiti all over London, chalked on every available wall. It was one of the few ways of avoiding the restrictions of the Newspaper Act which had made it very difficult for anyone who was not rich to produce a newspaper. Spence also produced cheap pamphlets which were sold on the streets by children, provoking the Duke of Portland at the Home Office to send out instructions to 'commit to the House of Correction little children selling Spence's halfpenny sheets'. The Spenceans were one of the few radical organizations to remain active during the repression of the previous decade and much of this was due to Spence's dogged determination to write and speak about his beliefs.

Tommy Spence was born in 1750 in Newcastle, of Scottish parents, and became a school teacher. He developed his idea of land nationalization as early as 1775. In 1792 he came to London where he set up his bookstall. He was considered by the Government to be a violent democrat and leveller, and was constantly harassed by spies and police. He was arrested

Thomas Spence

several times as a seditious author and for selling Tom Paine's *Rights of Man*, which was banned.

Spence supported the rights of women and children, including the right to easy divorce. He criticized colonial dispossession, especially of the American Indians and the Africans, and he argued for the land to be restored to the people. In 1801 he was tried for seditious libel, found guilty and sentenced to a year in Shrewsbury prison, with a fine of £20.

Wedderburn first saw him standing on a barrow in Oxford Street, a tankard of beer in his hand. He was only five feet tall, but sang loudly in a Geordie accent:

> *One night in my Bed,*
> *It came into my Head,*
> > *While locked up in Shrewsbury Jail;*
> *To send out Field Preachers,*
> *And Peaceable Teachers,*
> > *With Doctrines that never can fail.*

Bring bread and cheese and beer and let us sing cheerful songs and reason together. They cannot bear to see us endeavouring to act for ourselves. Do not men, when they meet, encourage each other and resolve each other's doubts and thus build one another up in their opinion? And cannot small meetings be effected where larger ones durst not be attempted? If but two or three meet together in so good a cause, a blessing will attend them.

Even under the modern tyrannies of China, France and Turkey, what could hinder small companies from meeting, in a free and easy manner, and singing their rights and instructing each other in songs? Can tyrants hinder people from singing at their work or in their families? If not, despair no longer, but begin immediately. Too much time has already been lost. Sing and meet, and meet and sing, and your chains will drop off like burnt thread.

> *Let's hear no more of despair,*
> *But sing your dear rights to each other,*
> *Till all think alike everywhere*
> *Even from one land's end to the other.*

The more I contemplate human affairs, the more I am convinced that a landed interest is incompatible with the happiness and independence of the world. All dominion is rooted and grounded in land and thence springs every kind of lordship which overtops and chokes all the shrubs and flowers of the forest. But take away those tall, those overbearing aristocratic trees, and then the lowly plants of the soil will have air, will thrive and grow robust.

Nevertheless take care you leave not any roots of those lordly plants in the earth, for though cut down to the stump like Nebuchadnezzar, yet if any vestige of the system remain, if any fibre of the accursed roots, though ever so small, lie concealed in the soil, they will sprout again and soon recover their pristine vigour, to the overshadowing and destruction of all the undergrowth.

> *May Afric's injured coast*
> *Soon have of this to boast,*
> *   The Rights of Man!*
> *Those rights from heav'n sent down*
> *Where no distinction's known*
> *Where black, or fair, or brown*
> *   Have equal claim.*

A WOMAN QUESTIONS THE ARISTOCRACY

Man over man made he not Lord

Spence's plan and full bellies

Wedderburn heard Spence speak on more than one occasion and helped to sell his pamphlets at his pitch in St Martin's Lane. This was near where Wedderburn lived, in Clare Market, off the Strand. Wedderburn would set up his handcart like a baker's van, with pamphlets displayed outside for customers to browse through, and clean copies available within. There also he did his tailoring work, patching clothes, whilst chatting to passers-by. Occasionally he blew a horn to attract customers.

Nearby, Billy Waters, a Black busker with a wooden leg, played the fiddle and collected halfpennies. He was dressed in a tattered shirt and wore a three-feathered hat decked with ribbons. While he played, another Black entertainer, Joseph Johnson, sang a nautical ditty to entertain the crowds in the street. In one hand he held a stick and he was supported under the other arm by a crutch. On his cap he had a model of a sailing ship and, when he swayed back and forth, the ship looked as if it was sailing on the ocean's waves. Next to them sat Dusty Bob. He had a placard on his breast, upon which was a wood-cut of a kneeling Black man, his wrists heavily chained, arms held high in supplication. Round the top of the picture was written *Am I not a man and a brother?*

When Joseph had finished, all three beggars joined in the song:

> *Of all the occupations,*
> *A beggar's life's the best;*
> *For whene'er he's weary,*
> *He'll lay him down to rest.*
> *And a begging we will go, we'll go, we'll go*
> *And a begging we will go.*

A customer approached Wedderburn's stall and, picking up a pamphlet, asked him, 'What's this *Rights of Infants* by Thomas Spence? I've heard of the rights of man and the rights of woman, but infants!'

Out of the corner of his eye, Wedderburn noticed two characters mounting the steps of St Martin's church and said to the customer, 'Look!' Some street theatre was about to begin.

Billy and the others continued their song:

Billy Waters, left, and Joseph Johnson

That all men are beggars, 'tis very plain to see:
Only some they are of lowly, and some of high degree.

A man, dressed up as a very fat, bloated aristocrat, stood on the top step sneering and turning up his nose. On a placard round his neck was written the word ARISTOCRACY. He took up the customer's question and addressed a fellow actress dressed in rags, 'And pray what are the Rights of Infants?'

The woman replied, 'They have a right to the milk of our breasts and we have a right to food to make milk of. They have a right to good nursing, to cleanliness, to comfortable clothing and lodging. Villain! Why do you ask that aggravating question? Have not the foxes holes, and the birds of the air nests, and shall the children of men have not where to lay their heads?'

Aristocracy sneered again, 'And is your sex also set up for pleaders of rights?'

The poor woman shouted, 'Yes, Moloch! Our sex were defenders of rights from the beginning. You shall find that we not only know our rights, but have spirit to assert them, to the downfall of you and all tyrants. And whereas we have found our husbands, to their indelible shame, woefully negligent about their own rights, as well as those of their wives and infants, we women mean to take up the business ourselves and let us see if any of our husbands dare hinder us. The natural fruits of the earth, being fruits of our undoubted common, we have indefeasible right to, and we will no longer be deprived of them.'

Aristocracy puffed himself up, 'Do you not, in lieu of those wild productions, get bread, and mutton, and beef, and garden stuff, and all the refined productions and luxuries of art and labour? What reason then have you to complain?'

The woman was indignant: 'Are you serious? Would you really persuade us that we have no reason to complain? Would you make us believe that we receive these productions of art and culture as a fair compensation for the natural produce of our common, which you deprive us of? Have we not to purchase these things before we enjoy them?'

'Sure, woman, you do not expect the fruits of men's labours and ingenuity for nothing! Do not farmers, in the first place, pay very high rents for their farms; and, in the next place, are they not at great trouble and expense in tilling and manuring the ground, and in breeding cattle? And surely you cannot expect that these men will work and toil, and lay out their money for you, for nothing?'

The woman responded: 'And pray, gentleman, who ever dreamt of hurting the farmers, or taking their provisions for nothing, except yourself? It is only the privileged orders, and their humble imitators on the highway, who have the impudence to deprive men of their labours for nothing. No, if it please your nobleness and gentleness, it is you, and not the farmers, that we have to reckon with. And pray now your highness, who is it that receives those rents which you speak of from the farmers?'

'We, to be sure, we receive the rents.'

'You, to be sure! Who the devil are you? Who gave you a right to receive the rents of our common?'

At this point Aristocracy drew out his sword and brandished it over the woman, 'Woman! Our fathers either fought for or purchased our estates.'

'Well confessed, villain! Now out of your own mouth will I condemn you, you wicked Moloch! And so you have the impudence to own yourself the cursed brood of ruffians who, by slaughter and oppression, usurped the lordship and dominion of the earth, to the exclusion and starvation of weeping infants and their poor mothers.

'O, you bloody landed interest! You band of robbers! Why do you call yourselves ladies and gentlemen? Why do you assume soft names, you beasts of prey? Too well do your emblazoned arms and escutcheons witness the ferocity of your bloody and barbarous origin! Your horrid tyranny, your infanticide is at an end! Your grinding the face of the poor, and your drinking the blood of infants, is at an end! The groans of the prisons, the groans of the camp, and the groans of the cottage, excited by your infernal policy, are at an end!

'And did you really think that you were the pillars that upheld the universe? Did you think that we would never have the wit to do without you? Did you conceive that we should never be able to procure bread and beef and fuel without your agency? Ah, my dear creature, the magic spell is broke. Your sorceries, your witchcrafts, your priestcrafts, and all your juggling crafts, are at an end.

'Moreover, when we begin with you, we will make a full end to your power at once. We will not foolishly tamper with the lion, and pluck out a tooth now and then, as some propose, to melt down your strength by degree, which would only irritate you to oppose us with all the power you had remaining.

'No, we will begin where we mean to end, by depriving you instantaneously of every species of revenue from lands, which will universally and at once be given to the parishes, to be divided fairly and equally among all the living souls, whether male or female, married or single, legitimate or illegitimate, from a day old to the extremest age. To labour for ourselves and infants we do not decline, but we are sick of labouring for an insatiable aristocracy!'

At the end of her speech there was tumultuous applause and cheering from the large crowd which had now gathered. The two actors bowed and went over to talk to Dusty Bob, while Billy and Joseph, sensing some more halfpennies coming their way, struck up their music and singing again.

Meanwhile Wedderburn asked his customer, 'Well, do you want to buy it?'

'Don't think so,' he replied. 'Sounds too dangerous to me. I might get nicked on the way home. Anyway my wife wouldn't like it.'

Accompanied by a spy, who was pointing at Wedderburn, a constable approached, saying, 'Have you got a licence?'

'What licence?'

The policeman rocked on his feet, 'Under the Hawkers and Pedlars Act you need a licence to sell things on the street. So, off, before you get arrested. You're causing an obstruction anyway and I've had my orders.' The few remaining customers disappeared quickly.

Picking up a pamphlet, the policeman continued, 'And these look like blasphemous and seditious pamphlets. The Rights of Infants! Whatever will they think of next?' He threw it to the ground and started destroying other pamphlets.

Wedderburn responded smartly, as if used to this procedure, and speedily wheeled his cart away.

Billy Waters saw the law approaching him too and responded, 'Can't a man earn an honest living by scraping cat-gut? Bah! Damme, me change my hotel tomorrow.' He took hold of Joseph's arm and strolled off singing:

> *Kitty, will you marry me,*
> *Kitty will you cry -*
> *Kitty, will you marry me,*
> *Kitty, will you cry - cry - cry!*

WEDDERBURN WRITES TO THE SLAVES OF JAMAICA AND TO HIS HALF SISTER, 1817

> **For who can tell but the millennium**
> **May take its rise from my poor cranium?**
> **And who knows but it God may please**
> **It should come by the West Indies?**

Thomas Spence died in September 1814 and was buried by about forty disciples, from whom the Society of Spencean Philanthropists was formed. In February 1817 the House of Commons Committee of Secrecy reported its concern that in the previous couple of years Spencean societies had multiplied among workers in the artisans' trades clubs, especially shoemakers, and also among discharged soldiers and sailors. A Parliament of landowners could imagine no greater crime than that of advocating they should be dispossessed of their land!

Also in 1817, dispossession of land - not in England, but in Jamaica - was on the mind of Robert Wedderburn, as he decided to write to the slaves of his native country:

Dear Countrymen,

Take warnings by the sufferings of the European poor and never give up your land you now possess, for it is your right by God and nature, for the earth was given to the children of men. Oh, ye Africans and relatives now in bondage to the Christians, because you are innocent and poor, receive this the only tribute the offspring of an African can give, for which I may ere long be lodged in a prison, without even a trial; for it is a crime now in England to speak against oppression.

Dear Countrymen, it is necessary for you to know how you may govern yourselves without a king, without lords, dukes, earls, or the like. The foundation of government should be this, that everything should be settled by votes throughout your nation. Choose a delegate to represent you, one for every 2,000, and change them once a year. Let ten years elapse before you send the same person again: a continual change will improve and qualify many of you to understand your laws and customs, and check that tyranny which is natural to man. Have no white delegate in your assembly. Never have a man worth more than five hundred a year.

Put no man to death for any crime, flog no body after fourteen years of age, nor cut off any nose nor ears, as is the practice in Jamaica. Let no man be pardoned who breaks your laws, let every individual learn the art of war, yea, even the females, for they are capable of displaying courage. You will have need of all your strength to defend yourself against those men who are now scheming in Europe against the blacks of San Domingo.

Have no lawyers amongst you; they cannot be honest in their profession. Have no barracks, but keep your arms and ammunition in your possession. Appoint inspectors to see that all are provided. Have no prisons; they are only schools for vice and depots for the victims of tyranny. Appoint a fool's cap to be worn at the age of five by everyone who knows not the alphabet. Let the alphabet be engraven on your trees and on every public wall, for knowledge is god-like strength which will regulate your physical force.

Again I say, have no lawyers amongst you. Every dispute may be decided in your own villages, by 12 men and 12 women. Let them be above fifty. Do not despise the judgement of old women, for they are generally clear in perceptions.

The island of Jamaica will be in the hands of the blacks within twenty years. Prepare for flight, ye planters, for the fate of San Domingo awaits you. You, my countrymen, all feel the injury; you are all capable of making resistance. But beware and offend not your God, like the Jews of old, in choosing a king; aggrandise no man by forms of law.

If you suffer any among you to become immensely rich, he will want homage and a title; yea, he will dispose of your lives, liberty and property; and, to support his divine right, he will establish a priesthood. He will call in foreign usurpers to assist him to oppress you. Under the protection *of foreign bayonets, he will threaten to erect a gallows at every door. France is reduced to this humiliation. A black king is capable of wickedness, as well as a white one.*

He also wrote the following letter to his sister:

Dear Miss Campbell,

When I heard of your kindness to my aged mother, it affected my whole frame, and made such an impression on my mind that I was at a loss to know which way to make you amends, but I soon accused myself for such a thought, when I recollected that it was a West Indian that performed the deed, who knows no merit in doing acts of humanity.

My dear Miss Campbell, be not alarmed or surprised, though you hold slaves, they must be let free, though sanctioned by the laws of England. Truth is my arrow stained with Africans' blood. Call your slaves together, let them form the half circle of a new moon, tell them to sit and listen to the voice of truth, say unto them...

'You were slaves to the cruel Spaniards, stolen from your country and brought here. Then Cromwell, the great, who humbled kings at his feet, and brought one to the scaffold, sent a fleet out, whose admiral dared not return without performing something to please his master. He came here and drove the Spaniards out and brought more slaves from Africa. Yes, the English, in the days of Cromwell, while they were asserting the rights of man at home, were destroying your ancestors then fighting for their liberty.

'I was tempted to purchase you as slaves, by the example of the white men, who are sanctioned by the English government, being void of shame. I am now instructed by a child of nature, to resign to you your natural right in the soil on which you stand, agreeable to Spence's plan. You are no longer slaves.

'I appeal to you. Forgive me. I have the written word of God to plead in my behalf. You are commanded to forgive. I confess my guilt. I have given up the wicked claim.

'The land is yours, not because Wedderburn, the Spencean, says so, for I have read the word of God, and it says, the Lord gave the earth to the children of men. You are the children of men as well as others. I can show no title deeds that are just. Those who sold it to me murdered them who lived on it before. I will manage it myself, as your steward; my brother will assist us. We shall live happy, like the family of the Shariers

Slave in irons

in the parish of St Mary's, who have all things common. We shall be like the Christians of old who attempted this happy mode of living in fellowship and brotherhood.'

Miss Campbell followed her brother's advice, but it was not easy, as this extract from her letter explains:

Dear Brother,

By setting my slaves free, and giving them the land, agreeable to Spence's plan, it has cast me into a gulph of trouble, for, when I went to have the deed recorded, the governor's secretary made a long pause, then told me he never heard of such a doctrine. He was not furnished with any legal form in which he could enter my will. He told me it was necessary the Governor should be acquainted with it. I was then brought before him. He looked at me with a pleasing steadiness and said:

'My dear, have you taken leave of your senses, to set your slaves free, and give them the land! Such an idea never entered the mind of anyone that ever existed who held land as private property and human beings as slaves. You must be in a state of delusion.'

Elizabeth replied, 'Oh no, sir, I am not. I was told to do it by my brother, and since I have done it I have felt my heart enlarged to love the whole human race. I can now keep the first and second commandment with joy. Yes, I now, indeed, love my neighbours as myself.'

The Governor became apoplectic: 'Hold your tongue, Miss Campbell, you have been listening to the Methodists.'

'I say, God bless the Methodists. They teach us to read the bible, and there it is written, that the slave which would not accept his liberty at the end of the seven years jubilee, must have his ears cut off, because he loved his master and mistress, and despised the law of liberty. He was never to have the benefit of another jubilee while he lived.'

The Governor turned to irony: 'Why, you have turned preacher, Miss Campbell. Where is your licence?'

'Why, sir, Jesus Christ and the apostles had their licence from God. I think it is a crime, sir, to ask a licence of any man to speak the truth, even at the risk of my life, as a Christian.'

The Governor became resigned, but issued a stern warning: 'Well, child, I will hear you on this head at a more convenient time, but, in the meanwhile, keep you slaves upon your own estate, for fear they should corrupt others and turn their brains to think that liberty and possession of the soil is better than slavery and the whip. There is a law made by the assembly to hang slaves. One has been hung for preaching, teaching or exhorting; another has been hung for throwing up his hoe and blessing the name of King George, through mistaking the abolition of the slave trade for the abolition of slavery.

'Your people, whom you have foolishly set free, are liable to the law till their freedom is recorded and then there is a fine of twenty pounds for each slave to whom they preached, for which they will be imprisoned. It is a pity but you could not wait fifteen or twenty years longer, for there will not be a white man on the island then.'

Elizabeth, however, was insistent: 'But, sir, the deed is done. I will obey you and keep them on our estate, but they have been talking about it this month past to the country negroes on market days. I told them not to speak of it, but they talked of it the more. The news is gone to Old Arbore and St Anns, to the Blue Mountains and to North Side, and the plantain boats have carried the news to Port Morant and Morant Bay. I hope, sir, they will not suffer for what they did in ignorance. Indeed had they attempted to keep it a secret, the oysters would have jumped off the trees.'

'Hold your foolish tongue and go home!'

Elizabeth curtsied and said firmly, 'Thank you, sir.'

The Governor turned aside and muttered to himself, 'There will be more white blood spilt in Jamaica than there was in San Domingo.'

When Elizabeth reached home, she continued the letter to her brother:

I have been told since, by a young gentleman, that the Governor had got a newspaper from England which gives an account of the Spencean doctrine. I could not believe him, but then he pulled out a newspaper from his pocket and read it to me. I was quite surprised to find that the good people of England were so much against the Spenceans. I thought the Blacks were the only objects of slavery and oppression. It is true what Solomon said, the rich hates the poor, no matter what the colour.

I, who am a weak woman of the Maroon tribe, understood the Spencean doctrine directly. I heard of it and obeyed and the slaves felt the force directly. They are singing all day at work about Thomas Spence and about you too, brother, and every time they say their prayers, they mention you.

We have heard of the weakness of the Prince Regent, and the wickedness of Castlereagh and Sidmouth, who imprison without crimes. God Almighty will set fire to them and burn up the wicked, both rich and poor; for the poor who side with the rich, as the instruments of oppression, will be destroyed. The poor that composed Pharaoh's army were all drowned in the Red Sea. Had they turned round and shot their officers, then fallen down on their knees and prayed to the God of Israel, Moses would have said to them, as he did to Jethro, come along with us and we will do thee good.

The free Mulattoes are reading Cobbett's Register and talking about San Domingo. A great many of the Spaniards fled here, you must know, and brought their favourite slaves with them from San Domingo, and the young men of Jamaica go amongst them, so they know the cause of their masters' coming to Jamaica.

The slaves begin to talk that if their masters were Christians they would not hold them in slavery any longer than seven years, for that is the extent of the law of Moses. The planters look frightened. The slaves know what it is about. They dare not speak, nor smile, for they would be hung for suspected conspiracy.

The Governor has ordered the assembly to meet directly to see what is to be done, but my sweetheart, who is a very sensible young man, says they can do nothing, for the leaven is laid too long in the dough, and as the slaves are their bread, they must not hang them all. I shall, if God spares my life, send you all the particulars respecting the assembly and the state of the island in general, in my next letter.

I send this letter by a black cook. I dare not trust it to the Post, for they open people's letters.

Your affectionate sister,

Elizabeth Campbell

A week later Elizabeth wrote another letter to Robert:

Dear Brother,

As I mentioned in my last letter, the meeting of the assembly took place and one, Mr Macpherson, said I should be considered a lunatic and be treated as such; for if the assembly was to countenance such a degree of madness, as to tolerate, by law, any individual giving liberty to their slaves, and a right to the soil, we should then become actual Spenceans.

This is Mr Macpherson's speech to the Jamaican Assembly:

Gentlemen, it would be as imprudent as allowing a man to set fire to his own house, in a city. Are we not all in jeopardy? It is your duty to act as the British Senators have done: suspend all laws, imprison the Spenceans, as madmen, and let the proprietors of the country arm themselves.

I would advise the House to send immediately to England for a million of gags, one million yards of chain, one million iron collars, and to send to Scotland for one hundred thousand starving Scotchmen to manage the slaves. And I recommend to this honourable assembly to petition my Lord Castlereagh to command the Prince to order them to withhold licences from all dissenting preachers, the Wesleyans in particular, and to call back to England all those that are in the island. And, unless our petition is attended to, I will recommend a revolt. There is no danger to be apprehended from any European power, for their strength is scarcely sufficient to keep their starving subjects in obedience to their will.

Gentlemen, it is time you should begin to act for your own safety. I have to inform this assembly that I am in possession of a tract called the Axe Laid to the Root, or a Fatal Blow to Oppressors, addressed to the Planters and Negroes of this Island. The tract is written by a native of this island, now in London, named Robert Wedderburn, and he has found means to convey them here.

The effect has been the cause of this meeting, to take into consideration the recording of the freedom and surrender of lands through the delusion of Spenceanism, which I oppose with all my soul, and earnestly solicit this House will decree, agreeable to the assertion of many able lawyers of the British House of Commons, that the Spenceans are madmen and ought to be treated as lunatics.

Therefore, I move that Miss Campbell be taken charge of as such, and her slaves and land be taken care of by the government, and place Mr Cruickshanks, the Negro-driver, for their overseer, and place a church parson over them, to eradicate, if possible, the Spencean delusion from their minds, and the false notion that freedom is better than slavery or the whip.

Elizabeth concluded her letter:

They have offered a reward for the 'Axe Laid to the Root' to be delivered up to the Secretary's office, by either slave or free man, but none have been delivered as yet.

I remain your affectionate sister,

Elizabeth Campbell

CHAPTER FIVE

HOPKINS STREET CHAPEL, 1819

Has a Slave the Right to Kill his Master?

To further his Spencean ideas, Robert Wedderburn opened a Unitarian chapel in Hopkins Street, Soho. 'Chapel' was a grand name for what was actually a dilapidated hayloft and what went on in that hayloft had little connection with most chapels!

Early on a Monday evening at the end of August, 1819, a cleaner from nearby St Giles could be found sweeping up the loft, picking up empty bottles and torn leaflets. In one corner stood some bales of hay which had obviously been sat upon, providing a balcony view of the proceedings. The walls were covered in slogans, daubed in bright colours:

EXUBERANCE IS BEAUTY

AN HOUR OF VIRTUOUS LIBERTY IS WORTH A WHOLE
ETERNITY OF BONDAGE

IF THE LION WAS ADVISED BY THE FOX, HE WOULD BE
CUNNING

EQUAL REPRESENTATION OR DEATH

WITHOUT CONTRARIES IS NO PROGRESSION

THE TERRITORY OF A NATION IS THE PEOPLE'S FARM

THE TYGERS OF WRATH ARE WISER THAN THE HORSES OF
INSTRUCTION

QUEEN MAB OR KILLING NO MURDER

UNIVERSAL SUFFRAGE AND ANNUAL PARLIAMENTS

KNOWLEDGE IS POWER

OPEN RESISTANCE OR UNCONDITIONAL SLAVERY

FOR CHILDREN AND WIFE,
WE WAR TO THE KNIFE!
SO HELP US GOD!

OUR RIGHTS - PEACABLY IF WE MAY, FORCIBLY IF WE
MUST

There were a few benches in the room and at one end a table standing on a dais. Behind this were hung pictures of Tom Paine and Toussaint L'Ouverture and beside them several flags - a skull and crossbones, a red, white and green tricolour, and a red flag.

The cleaner lent on her broom and surveyed the scene. Her mouth twisted and her eyes looked heavenward as she spoke to herself:

Right mess, ain't it? They call this a chapel too! Some chapel! Where I go is a proper chapel, a Methodist chapel with proper pews. We have a proper minister and proper hymns and prayers, not like this one. This minister, he calls himself Rev Wedderburn, but he's no proper minister. Goodness knows where he got his licence from!

He used to be a Methodist, but says we're too respectable for him now. What's wrong with respectability, I say. You certainly can't call him respectable. You should hear his language, and all the others, damnin' and blastin' all over the place. You wouldn't get away with that kind of language with Methodists.

And drink! Half of them are drunk when they arrive and the other half are drunk when they leave. How can they call it a chapel, with all the cursin' and swearin' that goes on. It's not proper. Blacks, Irish, soldiers, sailors, bricklayers, tailors, shoemakers, beggars - a right rabble. And they have animals in here too!

They say that the government sends spies here, and I'm not surprised. The things they talk about. It's enough to make your blood curdle. Look at this leaflet - 'Can it be murder to kill a tyrant?' Well, I mean, I'm no friend of Lord Castlereagh or Lord Sidmouth, but to murder them, no, no, no, that can't be right.

Listen to this - 'Has a slave a right to slay his master who refuses him liberty? The offspring of an African slave will open the question.' That's him, Rev Wedderburn, always going on about slavery. You'd think he'd been a slave himself, but he was free from birth, on account of his father was Scotch. Though he doesn't have much Scotch in him. More like gin or rum!

His father's disowned him completely, won't give him a penny. Once he travelled all the way up to Edinburgh, when he was out of work and his wife was pregnant, but his father just called him a lazy fellow and threatened to send him to jail. All he got was a draught of small beer from the cook and a cracked sixpence from the footman. Still, that's more 'n I get for cleanin' this place!

At this point she was interrupted by the trapdoor opening. Wedderburn's wife, Elizabeth, entered and asked, 'Have you finished yet?'

'Yes, I suppose so. It was in a dreadful mess. How can you call this a chapel? And all those things on the walls. That's not religion, that's politics, and dangerous politics at that.'

Elizabeth made a rude face behind the cleaner as she descended through the trapdoor and called out goodnight to her. There was no reply, so Elizabeth shrugged her shoulders. She lit some lamps and candles, as it was beginning to get dark, and set a chair near the entrance ready to collect the admittance fee of sixpence from those arriving.

The first to arrive was the chairman, Allen Davenport, shoemaker and poet. He was carrying an effigy of the Duke of Wellington which he placed beside him at the table. The trickle arriving became a flood, until the loft was crammed with about 200 people, all poorly dressed and all wearing white hats, tricolour cockades or caps of liberty. All, that is, except for two gentlemen, who sat at the back, well dressed and with their hats in their hands. These were immediately identified as the two spies, William Plush and Rev Eustace.

Last to arrive was Billy Waters, with a picture of Tommy Spence, which he hung on the wall. Dusty Bob started playing his fiddle and Billy danced a mime, while Joseph Johnson sang this song to the tune of God Save the King:

> *Hark! how the Trumpet's Sound*
> *Proclaims the Land around*
> *The Jubilee!*
> *Tells all the Poor oppress'd,*
> *No more they shall be tax'd,*
> *Nor Landlords more molest*
> *Their Property.*

Rents t'ourselves now we pay,
Dreading no Quarter-day,
　　　　Fraught with Distress.
Welcome that day draws near,
For then our rents we share,
Earth's rightful Lords we are,
　　　　Ordain'd for this.

Now hath the Oppressor ceas'd
And all the World releas'd
　　　　From Misery!
The Fir-trees all rejoice,
And Cedars lift their voice,
Ceas'd now the Feller's noise,
　　　　Long rais'd by thee!

The Sceptre now is broke,
Which with continual Stroke
　　　　The Nations smote!
Hell from beneath doth rise,
To meet thy Lofty Eyes,
From the most pompous size
　　　　Now brought to nought!

Since then this Jubilee
Sets all at Liberty
　　　　Let us be glad.
Behold each one return
To their Right, and their own,
No more like Doves to mourn
　　　　By Landlords sad!

After the applause died down, Wedderburn whispered something to Davenport, who then stood up and opened the meeting:

Good evening, citizens, and welcome to Hopkins Street Chapel.
Before the proceedings begin, I would like you to welcome Jack
Davies here. He used to be in the Life Guards, but has been
discharged without a pension. Bob found him yesterday in a starving
state down St Martin's Lane. He filled his belly and now he has
joined us Jacobins.

Please put your hands in your pockets and let us have your halfpennies, for soldiers also can assist us in our cause. Elizabeth, can you pass round a hat. Love the brave soldiers, for they are our brothers, natives of the same country, sufferers in the same calamities.

Now, I have great pleasure, tonight, to introduce to you two comrades from the West Indies who will contribute to our debate. Will you welcome, all the way from Kingston, Jamaica, Moses and Ephraim. We remember the words of Thomas Hardy, the founder of our old Corresponding Society: 'The rights of man are not confined to this small island, but are extended to the whole human race, black or white, high or low, rich or poor.' Before we start tonight's debate, I would like to ask Moses to say a few words.

Davenport sat down and there were cheers and shouts of welcome as Moses stepped on to the dais. He addressed the congregation like the Moses of old:

As soon as I became able to read, I discovered, in the holiest of all books, in the fountain of white men's religion; I discovered there, with a mixture of amazement and prophetic joy, that the very man, from who they had derived the name they had given me, of Moses, had been the happy deliverer of a nation.

What now will our task-masters pretend to object against the lawfulness of our revolt? If they our forefathers were slaves, so were the ancestors of those heroes, whom their Moses, their almost worshipped Moses, delivered from slavery.

Let them tell us, if they dare see truth, whether all the pomp, the pride, the wantonness, of that prosperity we see them live in, is not the purchase of our sweat, our tears and our distress?

Oh, my brethren in slavery, imagination, officious to torment me, invades my sleep with your shriekings. My very dreams are made bloody by your whips. I am insulted by the scoffs, the cruelties, the grinding, biting insolence, which we train up our poor children to the taste of. We have nothing but our shame to bestow on our posterity, nothing but the shame of our baseness, who have lengthened our slavery to out-last even life, by assigning them our children, on whom to practise their tortures.

But I have done with the horrors of this subject. Let us think then no more upon what we have suffered. Let us resolve to suffer no longer. Let us assure ourselves, that the proudest of our enemies will embrace us, in spite of our colour, when they foresee destruction in our anger, but ease and security in our friendship.

After more applause and cheering, Davenport thanked Moses and then adopted his poetic pose:

> *Too long, in unavailing tears,*
> *The supplicating Negro stood:*
> *Too long essay'd, with futile prayers,*
> *To stay the chast'ning hand of blood.*
>
> > *Tears, and submissive prayers, were vain!*
> > *His suff'rings pleas'd the tyrant train,*
> > *Who now, in trembling awe, shall feel*
> > *The vengeance of his last appeal.*
>
> *Ye winds, that oft the Negro's sighs*
> *To unregarding ears have borne;*
> *Ye waves, the witness to his cries,*
> *When from his home, his children torn.*
>
> > *To Europe's shores, with speed, away,*
> > *The shouts of vengeance now convey:*
> > *Bid its pale, guilty, despots hear*
> > *'The Negro's last appeal is War!'*
>
> *Fierce as their kindred whirlwinds wage,*
> *Fierce as the waves that rage return,*
> *The Sons of Afric claim the stage*
> *Of war, and for the contest burn.*
>
> > *Freedom, the prize for which they arm,*
> > *Displays each soul-inspiring charm:*
> > *And bids th'insluted Negro dare*
> > *Assert 'his last appeal is War!'*

The last line was repeated by the crowd as a chorus. The poet bowed and then calmed the congregation: 'Now let us begin our debate. The question tonight is: "Has a slave an inherent right to slay his master, who refuses him his liberty?" I call on our own Rev Bob Wedderburn, the black prince, to open the debate.'

A slave hung alive

At this the meeting erupted, with chants of 'black prince, black prince, black prince'. This is the man the crowd had come to hear, an orator who was famous throughout London. Wedderburn was now in his late fifties. His black hair was graying slightly and he had a cut across the bridge of his nose. He was only five feet five inches tall, but had an imposing presence, along with an impudent grin. It took a while before he could be heard above the tumult:

Most of you know that I am the offspring of an African slave. I am a West Indian and have experienced the horrors of slavery in Jamaica. My mother was bought and sold, flogged and raped. My grandmother, when she was 70 years old, was beaten almost to death. My brothers and sisters have been worked to death, tortured to death, burnt to death. All the horrors with which most of you are familiar are still going on, carried out by white Christian gentlemen.

But comrades, my fellow Africans have never failed to fight back. You have all heard of Bussa's rebellion in Barbados three years ago. And in the same year, as my good friends can confirm, over a thousand slaves were planning an insurrection in Jamaica, when they were betrayed.

Yes, they have spies in Jamaica too. The slaves were intended to effect a complete massacre of all the whites on the island. Their leader, the King of the Eboes, was captured and, with the militia under arms to prevent his escape, he was hanged at Black River. He died declaring that he left enough of his countrymen to prosecute the design in hand, and revenge his death upon the whites. Ephraim can vouch for this as he was there at Black River and he has promised me he will sing for us the song of the King of the Eboes.

Ephraim stood up and sang unaccompanied in a deep voice:

> *Oh me good friend, Mr Wilberforce, mek we free!*
> *God Almighty thank ye! God Almighty thank ye!*
> *God Almighty, mek we free!*
> *Buckra in dis country no mek we free:*
> *What Negro fe do? What Negro fe do?*
> *Tek force wid force! Tek force wid force!*
> *To be sure! to be sure! to be sure!*

The last two lines were repeated again and again with the congregation joining in. Wedderburn resumed his place:

Thank you, Ephraim. We need, however, to disabuse you about that old hypocrite Wilberforce. He does not think you are yet fit to bear emancipation. The obsolete old saint accepted the advice of Lord Castlefish, who cobbles at manacles for all mankind, and withdrew his registration bill. In the last twenty years that jesuit Mr Wilberforce, with his holy chatting, has done greater mischief than any other man in the curtailing of our liberties.

The aftermath of a slave revolt

Who more than the saintly Mr Wilberforce has clamoured against the reformers? He wishes to fasten the shackles of tyranny upon every hand at home and make whites the successors of blacks in the manacles of bondage.

What a pious man! He has supported every measure of the administration in the dungeoning, gagging, and transportation bills, against the reformers. A more contemptible and unprincipled hypocrite there is not in existence than this man. He is the humble servant of that cold-blooded vampire Castlereagh. As a member of the Society for the Suppression of Vice, he affects to check obscenity with one hand and scatters it most profusely with the other, in aiding the Prince Regent and his ministers.

At this point in the speech, Samuel Waddington, four feet high and known as the 'black dwarf', jumped on to the table and pretended to be Wilberforce. Wedderburn feigned surprise and then introduced him, 'I give you Mr Wilberforce, the ugly epitome of the devil.'

Waddington adopted a pose, as if doing a big speech in parliament:

It is necessary to pass this bill to prevent the confusion and utter ruin into which the nation is in danger of being plunged by the seditious societies which exist in its bosom. These societies, formed in the model of the Jacobin clubs in France, copying their proceedings, adopting their very phrases, as though the language of Great Britain is no longer fit to express their sentiments, and endeavouring to enlighten, as they term it, the public mind, are labouring, by every means that human ingenuity can devise, to defeat that established order of things so unfavourable to their wishes.

Books, prints, copper coins, expressive of their hatred and contempt of all authority, divine and human, are assiduously distributed, and clubs and debating societies multiply, where these sentiments are inculcated by inflammatory harangues. In short, it is impossible to conceive the ingenuity in mischief to which these men are prompted by that evil spirit now so busily at work to injure and distress this country.

A very considerable effect has been produced, I am grieved to say, by the unwearied exertions of these seditious men upon the minds of numbers, especially in and near the metropolis. These societies, it is true, mask their designs under the specious pretence of a parliamentary reform, but I am confident that I can prove to the conviction of every honest man, that it is no sort of reform of the present Government which will satisfy these bad men: nothing in short, but the total overthrow of the constitution.

I am possessed of information, from authentic documents, of the unwearied exertions of these bad men to sap the foundation of our comfort and hope as Christians and as members of society, and to destroy everything truly valuable both in this life and the next. These men sell poisonous compositions, such as 'The Rights of Man' and 'The Axe Laid to the Root'. We must put an immediate stop to this spreading evil, or it will be too late for ever. We must pass a bill for preventing seditious meetings and to prevent tumult and disorder.

Political discussion may yet take place. I should not have approved of any coercion, had the matter rested in mere speculative opinions, for these simply considered, are not in danger of producing great political changes, but in this instance we have seen them acted upon, and experienced their pernicious effects.

Another part of this bill relates to the prevention of debating clubs and lectures to which persons are admitted for money. Can the necessity of this be denied when, strange to tell, there are persons who actually make a trade of sedition, and seek to thrive by it as by a regular calling.

Those found guilty of stirring up a general hatred and discontent towards the law and constitution, and who show their incorrigible depravity and hardness of heart by repeating their crimes, should be banished into another land. They love not the British Constitution. They are at war, not with one branch of it only, the king, but equally so with each of the other branches, the Lords and the Commons; in short with everything that is beautiful and excellent in it; with all order, all property, all the best ties of this life and the hopes of another. In short, these bad men set themselves in array against God and man.

> *My friends, in an ocean of troubles I've been -*
> *By the people I'm laughed at, - despised by the Queen*
> *And many there are who presume to make clear*
> *That Lord Sidmouth and I are not over sincere;*
> *They say that our piety's nothing but cant,*
> *And all our fine speeches mere tragedy rant!*
> *To the poor we've sent Bibles, which ought to be read,*
> *But never once thought that they languished for bread!*
> *Oh! what will be said to our praying and preaching?*
> *I'm afraid we don't practise the doctrines we're teaching.*

The whole speech was accompanied by ironic jeers and heckling from the audience, but Waddington's large voice in a small body easily carried the day. Wedderburn helped him down off the table and said with a smile, 'Remember Cobbett's list of things he wouldn't miss, when he ran away to America? His greatest consolation was "No Wilberforce! think of that! no Wilberforce!"'

Ephraim indicated that he wanted to speak again and Wedderburn beckoned him up. In a serious tone he said: 'I will take back to Jamaica your views on Mr. Wilberforce. But please listen to mine of the subject of slavery. You have mentioned Bussa's rebellion in Barbados. One white man was killed by the rebels, yet in revenge almost three hundred Blacks were killed in battle or executed. Christians who treat men like beasts prove that their religion is no more than a grimace. For simply running away, my sister Priscilla had both her ears cut off close to her head. She had to suffer 39 lashes on the first Monday in every month for a whole year, as well as being worked in irons during that time. I say, "Take force with force."'

Wedderburn took up the refrain and continued his speech:

Take force with force. Fight fire with fire. When Captain Rivington was tried for hanging a girl by each limb, for twenty minutes, then throwing her down the ladder of the after hatchway, and in the morning she was found dead, on the spot where she fell, this was the evidence given upon oath. Yes, and in the presence of our prince, the admiral,

Maroon warrior

the prisoner acknowledged to the deed, but contended that it was but five minutes, and not twenty!

The witness was imprisoned for perjury and the captain acquitted, for he satisfied the court, in his defence, that severe means were necessary to be used to cure the slaves of the sulks, who frequently would not eat, which endangered the merchant's interest in the cargo, for unless they appear in good condition at market they would not fetch a price.

This captain rode in triumph, with a crowd of sailors with blue ribbons in their hats, and met his Christian employers, the slave-trading merchants of Bristol, who rejoiced that killing a black was no murder.

Take force with force. The government sent forces to Africa and the West Indies to steal our brothers and sisters for gain, just as parliament *men employ women and children in their cotton factories and make slaves of them for money. And should we not resist? Should we accept the violence of hunger, the violence of homelessness, the violence of oppression, the violence of slavery and not resist? When that damned rascal Lord Sidmouth censors our publications, imprisons our members without trial, bans our processions and demonstrations, puts up the price of bread, refuses our petitions, and sends spies amongst us, should we not resist?*

To lay the axe to the root, and treat the subject under consideration with candour, those jumping monkeys in their pulpits tell us to be quiet like that bloody spooney Jesus Christ, who like a bloody fool tells us when we get a slap on one side of the face, turn gently round and ask them to smack the other! I prefer jolly old Peter with his rusty sword.

This is reason, sweet reason. Who can believe the bible anyway? It is full of contradictions and certainly ought not to be admitted as evidence in a court of justice. Does not Jesus also say, 'I come not to send peace, but a sword.' Matthew chapter 10, verse 34. 'He that hath no sword, let him sell his garment and buy one.' And in Exodus chapter 21, verse 16: 'And he that stealeth a man, and selleth him, or if he be found in his hand, he shall surely be put to death.' And in Jeremiah chapter 22, verse 13: 'Woe unto him that buildeth his house by unrighteousness, and his chambers by wrong; that useth his neighbour's service without wages, and giveth him not for his work.'

That's why we say, 'Take force with force.' They have declared war against us, and should we not resist? Should we not avenge the horrid massacre at Manchester? Should we not avenge the poor woman whose infant was drenched in its mother's blood? If the executive power denies justice to the inhabitants of Manchester, the people have but one resource left: the duty of the people will then be to go armed to public meetings. The revolution has already begun in blood there, with the cuttings, choppings, and killings at Manchester, and it must now also end in blood here. If we can't all get arms, there's them iron railings in front of these big fellows' houses: these will supply some with arms.'

Will Englishmen any longer suffer themselves to be trod upon like the poor African slaves in the West Indies?

> *Petitioning for pity is most weak,*
> *The sovereign people ought to demand justice.*

Nothing but a revolution can remove a deep-rooted corruption, hence revolutions are much to be desired when necessary.

Reason and common sense should be our guide. An unnecessary shedding of blood is at all time to be deprecated, but circumstances will occur when it is found to be indispensable. Show me a state of oppression and despotism that was ever overthrown by the weapons of reason alone, and I for one will be forced to acquiesce in pacific reasoning. Did reason prevent the legalised murders at Derby or the inhuman unparallelled butcheries at Manchester? Remember the words of the creature in Frankenstein: 'I was benevolent and good; misery made me a fiend.'

For my part, old as I am, I am learning my exercise as a soldier. I have been taught how to handle small arms on the top station of a privateer, but I still think it necessary to practise drilling and manoeuvres. I would rather die like Cashman, the Irish sailor, than live like a slave. But before I die, I would have the satisfaction of plunging a dagger into the heart of a tyrant. Think of the horrid butcheries that took place in Ireland. May the carcasses of tyrants rot like dung upon the face of the earth and become manure for the roots of the tree of liberty.

I have written a letter to the Prince Regent, that great fat dandy in Pall Mall.

This was the signal for Samuel Waddington to jump up on the table again, dressed in a purple robe. Meanwhile Billy Waters sang a song:

> *'Tis in Pall Mall there lives a Pig,*
> *That doth this Mall adorn,*
> *So fat, so plump, so monstrous Big,*
> *A finer ne'er was born.*

> *This Pig so sweet, so full of Meat,*
> *He's one I wish to kill.*
> *I'll fowls resign, on thee to dine,*
> *Sweet Pig of fine Pall Mall.*

As Wedderburn resumed his speech, Waddington acted the part of the Prince of Wales in mime, to the jeers and cheers of the crowd.

To His Royal Highness George, Prince of Wales, Regent. Sire, I have watched your propensities from the age of eighteen to the present time. I cannot account for my so doing, for I was then a stranger in the country, and being a foreigner I knew nothing of you before that period. I am fully persuaded you are no more than a man.

I ask without ceremony, why was Pharaoh's house troubled? Why was the first born of Egypt slain? Why was the hope of propagating their race blasted by the eternal God? It was for holding men as slaves and monopolizing the land.

Let the slaves go free, for it is their right. Free them. Napoleon has set the pattern. Remember vengeance belongeth unto God; he will arise and execute justice and judgement. Shall the cause which produced destruction to the house of Pharaoh and his nation fail to produce the same effect, where similar crimes exist? The law of nature, which is the law of God, is uniform in its operations. The suit of clothes that fitted that nation may be worn by another of the same description, says the immortal Paine.

Job confessed that his sins sat about his neck like the collar of his coat. I give this simile, being a tailor, and if report speaks true, you are well acquainted with the science of cutting and fitting yourself with a coat.

I remain, till death, in strict sincerity and obedience, Robert Wedderburn.

P.S. I have a present to give you next time you are passing by Hopkins Street. It is this elegant snuff box. As you know, that petrified putrefaction, Lord Castlebrag, has spent £22,000 of our money this year to buy snuff boxes to present to foreign ministers. This one is special, however, for it is decorated with various revolutionary emblems, in particular the head of Charles the First... and an axe!

Wedderburn made to present the snuff box to Waddington who flicked it violently from his hand and addressed him in haughty manner:

Dear Bob, if I may call you Bob, I care not a fig for your snuff box. And as long as I have two or three whores and plenty of wine, I don't care a damn about the people's sufferings either. My mad father'll be dead soon and then I'll be king.

Now bugger off back to Jamaica where you belong, you devil's engineer. We've got far too many blackies here as it is, all promoting sedition and treason. Or go to France and join the bloody Jacobins. And all these damned Irish navvies all over the place too. Why don't they go back where they came from?

I must say this is a very strange chapel and your congregation is a most contemptible rabble. It is full of the lowest class of people: disbanded soldiers and sailors, broken-down butchers and starving shoemakers. I can only see two worshippers who look half way decent, with their hats in their hands. Look at the rest. They've all got their hats on. What a set of ignorant ragamuffins!

At this mock incitement the audience cheered and threw their hats in the air, whilst the two spies looked decidedly uncomfortable at the back of the room. Wedderburn quickly put on a black cloak and pretended to be a priest:

Lord, we beseech thee, to defend George, Prince of Wales, our present Regent, from battle and murder and sudden death; and from fornication and all other deadly sins.

O Prince, ruler of the people, have mercy upon us, thy miserable subjects.

From the blind imbecility of ministers, Good Prince deliver us.

From all deadly sins attendant on a corrupt method of election, Good Prince deliver us.

From taxes levied by distress, from jails crowded with debtors, from poor-houses overflowing with paupers, Good Prince deliver us.

From conspiracies against the liberties of the people, Good Prince deliver us.

From utter starvation, Good Prince deliver us.

Waddington spurned the priest: 'Petition me no petitions.' Both actors then bowed and Wedderburn did another quick change into the supercilious Sidmouth, to the hisses and boos of the spectators. Davenport pointed to him and announced, 'Behold Lord Viscount Sadmouth, a driveller, a bigot, a knave without shame!'

Then Wedderburn and Waddington played out a poetic scene between Sidmouth and the Prince Regent.

Wedderburn: 'Tis pity that these cursed State Affairs
Should take you from your pheasants and your hares
Just now:
But lo!
CONSPIRACY and TREASON are abroad.

Waddington: *Check the circulation of little books*
                    Whose very looks -
                    Vile 'two-p'nny trash' - bespeak abomination

Wedderburn: *Oh! they are full of blasphemies and libels*
                    And people read them oftener than their bibles!

Waddington: *Reform, Reform, the swinish rabble cry -*
                    Meaning, of course, rebellion, blood, and riot -
                    Audacious rascals! you, my Lord, and I,
                    Know 'tis their duty to be starved in quiet:
                    But they have grumbling habits, incompatible
                    *With the repose of **our** august community -*

Wedderburn: *Yes, they declare*
                    That we are not God's favourites alone -
                    That they have rights to food, and clothes, and air,
                    As well as you, so brilliant on your throne!
                    Oh! indications foul of revolution -
                    The villains would destroy the Constitution!

Waddington's tone as the Prince of Wales became more colloquial, 'Speaking of villains, don't you remember how we freed the slaves held by that villain, the Dey of Algiers?'

Wedderburn resumed his true self and expostulated to Waddington: 'What grounds have you got to boast of relieving the slaves of Algiers, when you, as a Christian prince, practise the same? What grounds have the clergy of the Church of England to punish people for publishing parodies of the ceremonies of their church, while they allow their brethren to hold my relations as slaves? Is it not straining at a gnat, while they swallow a camel? How can the House of Commons pride themselves of possessing greatness, when they frame the laws to authorize their priests and princes to hold my relations as slaves? Can that be right in our princes and priests which is wrong in the Dey of Algiers and the priests of Mahomet?'

Waddington was still playing the prince and reacted in anger: 'You dung tailor! My tailor is a very fine tailor, not a dung tailor like you.' Wedderburn pretended to strangle him, as he turned to Davenport: 'And as for my shoemaker, all shoemakers are damned rascally radicals...'

There was uproar and laughter as the mock fight continued. Davenport exclaimed, 'Now you've gone too far, you great booby!' He banged his gavel on the table to try and restore order and pointed at Waddington. Another poetic scene ensued.

Davenport: *When I gaze*
On the proud palace, and behold one man
In the blood-purpled robes of royalty,
Feasting at ease, and lording over millions,
Then turn me to the hut of poverty,
And see the wretched lab'rer worn with toil,
Divide his scanty morsel with his infants,
I sicken, and indignant at the sight,
Blush for the patience of humanity.

Waddington: *I am a prince - by nature I am noble:*
These fields are mine, for I was born to them.
I was born in the palace - you, poor wretches,
Whelp'd in the cottage, are by birth my slaves!

Wedderburn: *This is the man, all shaven and shorn,*
All cover'd with Orders, and all forlorn;
The dandy of sixty
who bows with a grace,
And has taste in wigs, collars,
cuirasses and lace;
Who, to tricksters and fools,
leaves the state and its treasure,
And, when Britain's in tears,
sails about at his pleasure:
Who spurn'd from his presence
the friends of his youth,
And now has not one
who will tell him the truth.

Davenport: *We are all equal; nature made us so.*
Equality is our birth-right.
When Adam delv'd and Eve span,
Who was then the gentleman?

Waddington jumped to the floor to raucous applause and Davenport said, 'Bob, the floor is yours again and the table is mine.' Wedderburn bowed mockingly to Davenport and addressed the congregation:

Thank you, Mr Chairman. As you know, I am a flint tailor and know how to patch clothes, and looking round here, I see that there is plenty of work to be done. But in the end, when the cloth is worn out, the coat has to be cast into the fire. It can be mended no longer. Such is England's coat today. No more patching, no more mending, no more repairing.

The rich are always enemies of the poor; they despise us. They not only despise us themselves, but they teach their servants to do so. A hideous system exists on the part of the powerful, the rich, and the religious, to punish and persecute every indication of happiness that is seen among the labouring part of the community. In some factories slavery is quite systematic. If the negroes abroad are subject to a driver with a whip, the same is practised at home; and regular floggers are a part of the establishment in our great factories in the north. Fines attend the slaves at every step, and to be found reading aught but a religious tract is a disqualification for further employ.

Some say that we ought not to blame our governors, for their ignorance produces errors by which we are misguided; but, are they willing to be taught? No. Then what ought to be done? I dare not tell you, but I know what they ought to do to me if I was steering a gilded yacht which they were in, and through ignorance was likely to run her on a rock. What would they do if I was determined to persevere? It would be their duty to place a wiser man at the helm. If I refused to quit the helm they ought to blow my brains out, for it is better for one to die than the whole perish, not because of guilt, but matter of prudence and sound policy.

You will not charge me with want of philosophy, for surely it is wisdom in the gardener to prune the vine as long as pruning is useful, but when the vine proves rotten, it is necessary to tear it up by the root, for why cumbereth it the ground?

'And now also the axe is laid unto the root of the trees: every tree therefore which bringeth not forth good fruit is hewn down, and cast into the fire.' Luke chapter 3, verse 9. Corrupt the fruit, corrupt the tree, and most corrupt the root. This country is a barren tree. It needs to be hewn down and burnt in a purifying fire. Then a phoenix will rise again from the ashes.

What will this new land be like? It will be the people's farm, for 'the territory of a nation is the people's farm' as Tommy Spence used to say.

> *Thus all the world belongs to man,*
> *But not to kings and lords;*
> *A country's land's the people's farm,*
> *And all that it affords:*

> For why? divide it how you will
> 'Tis all the people's still:
> The people's country, parish, town;
> They build, defend and till.

The doctrine of the Spencean is simple and easy to understand. It has its foundation in the laws of nature, for as man cannot exist without subsistence, nature has given the earth for that purpose. But mankind have been deprived of their natural rights to the soil, and he that first thrust his brother from this right was a tyrant, a robber, and a murderer; a tyrant, because he invades the rights of his brother; a robber, because he seized upon that which was not his own; a murderer, because he deprives his brother of the means of subsistence.

The weak then must solicit to become the villain's slave. The descendants of these ruffians saw the necessity of making laws for preserving their ill-gotten possessions, and punishing those who are bold to claim their natural right to the soil. And upon this fraudulent principle society is constructed. Those usurpers of the soil, giving themselves titles, demanding submission of those whom they have robbed, the greatest robber is chosen for their king, to guarantee the rest their possession. The Scots lairds who, when called upon to show their title deeds to their estates, drew their swords, were consistent with the actions of the original despoilers.

Private property in land has been the cause of all the blood which has been shed for this last fifty years. Had every man in France partook of the share of rents of their native soil, Louis XVI might have worn his head a little longer, and the present Louis would have no occasion for a standing army of foreigners to keep him on the throne.

The Spenceans say that force ought not to be used in an enlightened age; argument is the weapon to be recommended. But are we living in an enlightened age and is argument enough? Has argument changed the situation in Ireland? Oh ye poor of Ireland, your death, through starvation, will be a perpetual, yea an eternal monument of disgrace to the landholders; it will be an immortal book, wherein will be read the wicked system of private property in land.

But Britons have not lost the spirit of their fathers: hence the necessity of a standing army in the time of peace. Don't degrade the English nation; they are capable of destroying the usurpers of their rights. The British tars, though ignorant and more degraded than the West Indian slaves, display agility, skill, and valour superior even to the sailors of the French Republic. I have been a witness myself, on board the Poliphemus, when *the ship's cook and the cook's mate of the Ward room were being flogged for taking an extra drop of grog, before the combined fleet, in sight of Gibraltar. Thoughtless of their bloody backs, they engaged the common enemy of their country, France and Spain.*

The British sailors will have a greater motive to excite them when they are entitled to a share of the rents. When they return, their families will not be induced to hide them from a pressgang; no, they will push them forward in their country's cause, knowing the land will then be worth defending, being the property of the people. They will say, like the Britons and Romans of old, return victorious or not at all.

Will not the females assist, if necessity requires? Yes, the tender passion of a mother will compel her to defend her children's share of rents. I hope, citizens, you are convinced that England is capable of defending herself under the Spencean influence of enthusiasm. Once we have got rid of the landlords, we will never allow those overgrown fat leeches to return.

The press is our other resource. We must write for the poor. How can that be better done than in the exposure of all written errors which oppress them? What is the use of any other writing for the poor than that which will remove those priests and that aristocracy which press them to the earth? They may burn, by the hand of the common hangman, Mr Carlile's publications of Paine's 'Rights of Man', but they cannot burn it out of my head.

In 'The Axe Laid to the Root' I have written to my sister in Jamaica to free her slaves. We must also prepare pamphlets to be sent to India to those suffering Blacks, to open their eyes that they might strike for their long lost liberty. I am an oppressed, insulted and degraded African. I am also a West Indian, a lover of liberty, and would dishonour human nature if I did not show myself a friend to the liberty of others.

The end of Wedderburn's speech was greeted with cheers and many hats thrown in the air. Wedderburn smiled and took up his glass of ale, ready for the toasts which usually ended the meeting. He sat down, to be replaced by Davenport who again adopted his poetic stance to quote from Shelley's 'Queen Mab':

> *From kings, and priests, and statesmen, war arose,*
> *Whose safety is man's deep unbettered woe,*
> *Whose grandeur his debasement. Let the axe*
> *Strike at the root, the poison tree will fall;*
> *And where its venomed exhalations spread*

> Ruin, and death, and woe, where millions lay
> Quenching the serpent's famine, and their bones
> Bleaching unburied in the putrid blast,
> A garden shall arise in loveliness
> Surpassing fabled Eden.

Men who are excluded from the land, or the profits therefrom, are like beautiful and blooming flowers suddenly snatched from their genial beds: they fade, wither, and prematurely die. The land is the people's farm. Under Spence's plan the labouring classes will no longer have the gloomy prospect of bringing up their children to be thieves and prostitutes. I propose a toast to Tommy Spence:

> 'Tis liberty alone, that gives the flow'r
> Of fleeting life its lustre and perfume;
> And we are weeds without it.

Let the political principles of Paine and the divinity of Carlile be our object, and ere long we shall silence all enemies who dare make head against us. To the liberty of the press and freedom of discussion. May the skin of tyrants be burnt into parchment and the Rights of Man written upon it. I give you the immortal Paine and the equality of man.

> Off with your fetters; spurn the slavish yoke;
> Now, now, or never, can your chain be broke;
> Swift then rise and give the fatal stroke.

To the downfall of oppression, and may tyranny be buried in its ruins. I give you Dr Johnson's toast: To the next slave rebellion in the West Indies.

> Now to ARMS let each poor man fly!
> Let Freedom live AND TYRANTS DIE!
> Arch-Fiends have Civil War begun:
> Death to the wretch that now would run!

Justice without a mask, and liberty without restraint.

> Rise, unite, demand reform,
> Let no tyrant you alarm,
> And if refus'd, then let us arm
>   And fight for liberty.

Toussaint L'Ouverture

I give you Toussaint L'Ouverture and the 'Mingo rebellion. War has already been declared against us. Why then should we hesitate? For my part I am ready now. I compare the present time to the crisis of the French Revolution; we must arm ourselves as they did. If slaves in San Domingo can win their freedom, so can slaves in Jamaica and slaves in England. I call on all those in support of the resolution to raise their hands.

A forest of hands flew into the air and there were cries of 'All!' But then someone indicated the spies at the back of the room and all eyes turned on them. One raised his hand tentatively. The other began to raise his too, but by then the first one had put his hand down again. For a moment they operated like a piston going up and down, and the whole congregation laughed in derision. The spies made a hasty retreat and disappeared down through the trapdoor. The jeers turned to cheers and Davenport called out, 'I declare the resolution carried unanimously.'

Wedderburn concluded, 'I can now write home and tell the slaves to murder their masters as soon as they please!' There was more laughter and throwing of hats in the air. Davenport set fire to the effigy of the Duke of Wellington. This was the signal for Billy Waters to strike up on his fiddle and sing the finale to the tune of 'God Save the King':

> *Gory is Europe's plain,*
> *Whelmed beneath her slain,*
> *Dreadful to see.*
> *Bleeding promiscuously,*
> *Victors and vanquish'd lie,*
> *Mingled in butchery,*
> *Let man be free.*
>
> *Long live great guillotine,*
> *Who shaves the head so clean,*
> *Of queen or king;*
> *Whose power is so great,*
> *That ev'ry tool of state,*
> *Dreadeth his mighty weight,*
> *Wonderful thing!*
>
> *Hasten the happy day,*
> *When Reason's heavenly ray*
> *Dares to be free;*
> *Priestcraft shall hide its head,*
> *Kings be remembered*
> *Only in tales of dread,*
> *Sweet liberty.*

The next day was a Tuesday and in the cold light of a warm summer's day the spy, Rev Chetwode Eustace, was still shaking inside and out. He sat at his desk and wrote this letter to the Home Secretary:

Dear Lord Sidmouth,

Yesterday evening I proceeded to Hopkins Street Chapel to hear the question discussed whether it be right for the people of England to assassinate their rulers, for this, my Lord, I conceive to be the real purport of the question, though proposed in other terms.

I had some difficulty to discover the place, for it is a ruinous loft which you ascend by a step-ladder. The assemblage was perfectly suitable to the place, for both orators and audience were, with a few exceptions, persons of the very lowest description.

The doctrines were certainly of the most dreadful nature, and two persons particularly distinguished themselves by expressions which appeared to me the most violently seditious and treasonable. One of these men, who appeared to be the principal in their concern, is a mulatto and announced himself as the descendant of an African slave.

After noticing the insurrections of the slaves in some of the West India Islands, he said they fought in some instances for twenty years for liberty. And he then appealed to Britons who boasted such superior feeling and principles, whether they were ready to fight now but for a short time for their liberties. He stated his name to be Wedderburn and said he was the author of a production entitled 'The Axe Laid to the Root' or some such name.

Your Lordship will perceive that these persons are of the most contemptible description. However, I fear they are too successful in their efforts to corrupt the lower orders. From what I have observed of these fellows, I would most humbly recommend that some proper persons may be sent to watch their proceedings, and that prompt measures may be adopted for making examples of Wedderburn and such desperate characters who so fearlessly violate the laws and avow their object to be nothing short of the assassination of their rulers and the overthrow of the government.

I have the honour to be, with the highest respect, my Lord, your Lordship's most obedient, humble servant, Rev Chetwode Eustace.

P.S. Should it be your Lordship's wish at any time to see me, you will be pleased to have a note directed to the case of Mr Stockdale, Pall Mall.

SHOULD THE METHODISTS PREACH PASSIVE OBEDIENCE TO THE SLAVES?

The following day in the early evening the cleaner of Hopkins Street Chapel could be found again grumbling at the mess she had to clean up:

Look at the state of this place. It looks like they had a bonfire here and it's still two months till Guy Fawkes day. It's a wonder the place didn't burn down.

I've heard that the Rev Wedderburn's been arrested. Accused of superstitious libel, they say. Listen to this leaflet:

Says Harry to Dick, 'Come, lad, be of good cheer!
The Government soon will be changed as I hear.'
'Good news!' replies Dick; 'but it better would be,
If in CHANGED you'd fairly omit letter C.'

They want to hang the government! I'm not surprised he's been arrested.
We're taught in our Methodist chapel to honour and obey the government,
pay our taxes and, as John Wesley said, 'No smuggling.' 'Render unto
Caesar the things which are Caesar's.' Know what I mean? Don't mix
politics and religion. Otherwise you'll see where it gets you.

He'll end up being hanged himself, if he's not careful. Look what
happened to that Irish fellow Cashman. And they claim we're too
respectable. What's wrong with being respectable? I'd rather be
respectable than end up dangling on the end of a rope!

As she finished sweeping up, Elizabeth's head appeared above the trap
door. She came into the loft and the cleaner hurried to descend. Elizabeth
wished her good night, but there was no response. 'So much for Methodist
fellowship!' she muttered.

She set up the table to collect the money and the congregation quickly
assembled. This time the spy, William Plush, was accompanied by
Matthew Matthewson, instead of Rev Eustace. There was no sign of
Wedderburn, but Billy Waters got the proceedings under way by singing
'The Digger Song':

Your houses they pull down, stand up now, stand up now,
Your houses they pull down, stand up now.
Your houses they pull down to fright poor men in town,
But the gentry must come down, and the poor shall wear the
crown.
Stand up now, Diggers all.

Their self-will is their law, stand up now, stand up now,
Their self-will is their law, stand up now.
Since tyranny came in, they count it now no sin
To make a gaol a gin, to starve poor men therein.
Stand up now, stand up now.

Davenport took the floor: 'Welcome, citizens. The bad news is that, though
our Black Dwarf is here, our Black Prince has been arrested for seditious
libel.' There were boos and groans all round, until Davenport intervened:

'The good news, however, is that he has been acquitted by the jury.' The ensuing cheering grew even louder as Wedderburn appeared through the trapdoor, kissed Elizabeth and took his seat on the platform.

Davenport continued: 'Our topic for tonight is - Which is the greater crime: for the Wesleyan missionaries to preach up passive obedience to the poor black slaves in the West Indies; or to extort from them at the rate of £18,000 per annum, under the pretence of supporting the gospel. I call upon Bob to open the debate.'

Wedderburn smiled and rose to address the meeting:

Thank you, comrade. First let me say how glad I am to be here again tonight and out of the clutches of the Doctor, that rascally bugger Sidmouth. His tentacles stretch across the land, but fortunately we still have our London juries. Little Waddie, our little bill-sticker here, has already been acquitted twice on charges of exhibiting seditious placards. But I fear the next time may not be so easy for either of us.

To the matter in hand – Wesleyan missionaries. Those vipers of church missionaries sent out by our villainous state to suck the blood of the poor innocent blacks in the West Indies and make them believe that the great God is with them. The devil rather !

The devil and the missionaries have been sent, for no other purpose than to extort money from the blacks and preach passive obedience to them. These villains are no better than thieves. If the slaves have no money to give these church robbers, they are tied up and flogged most unmercifully. Isn't that so, Ephraim?

Ephraim nodded vigorously and offered up an ironic prayer: 'O Lord, I thank thee for sending big ship to my country, and wicked men to steal me and bring me here that I might know and love thee.' The congregation erupted in laughter.

Not to be outdone, Waddington intoned a credo: 'I believe in Lord Castle in the Air, the Supreme Director of all our affairs, maker of treaties for all nations, for the benefit of none; and in the excellence of his features, fundamental... and unfundamental.' At the mention of fundamental Waddington pulled down his trousers and showed his bum to the audience which hooted in derision.

Wedderburn continued with his speech:

Fellow citizens, that Derry Down Triangle and Irish Rat Catcher supported the Corn Bill, which was aimed at poor people's guts and lined the pockets of church and state and the great landowners. But what did those damned infernal villains care as long as they got their rents from their tenants? The poor could go to hell. Is not that great booby in Pall Mall ashamed of himself to have been led by the nose by his ministers for so long? The country has stood it too long. Mr Carlile has opened the eyes of the whole of the United Kingdom of Great Britain and they are awake to the villainy that is practised every hour and every day. God send us better days: we cannot have worse. But God, I think, has nothing to do with it. He too has forsaken us altogether.

'Give us this day our daily bread' is a prayer that may suit a set of lazy priests, but we all know that the honest man may have it if he will earn it, that is, if he be so situated as to find profitable employment. It will never come by prayer. Let us gird on the shield of reason and drive these drones from our hives.

I have written a letter to Parson Charley: 'To the most reverend the Lord Archbishop of Canterbury. My Lord, God is love: he that dwelleth in love, dwelleth in God, and God in him, for the love of God is shed abroad in our hearts, if we are Christians. By the holy spirit, this love evinces itself by a manifestation of benevolence to the brethren. That you possess this love is beyond the possibility of a doubt.

'When, at your palace in Lambeth, you hear the cries of your Christian brethren, and see them expose the secrets of nature, for want of clothing, surely you must be prepared to sacrifice the whole of your immense income, and reduce yourself to the state of your humble master. Yea, your palace could be sold to feed and clothe the hungry and naked, though such an act would leave you as destitute as the apostle Paul. You would bear the hardships of hunger and cold. Such conduct would illuminate the world and set religion on high. It would show the infidels their deficiency; they would be compelled, seeing your good works, to glorify your father which is in heaven.

'Recollect Elijah and the widow: she gave to the hungry prophet her last cake. The Lord rewarded her with an abundance. And if you were to discover an act of this kind, all the accusers of Christian priests would be confounded, and the starving inhabitants, your neighbours, would burst forth in acclamations of joyous praise to the Deity. Amen.'

The congregation responded with ironic amens. Waddington assumed the guise of the Archbishop and lambasted Wedderburn: 'You great nincompoop! Can you seriously imagine me selling my palace to provide food and clothing for a dung tailor like you. These street ragamuffins which I see around me deserve a whipping, not charity. They are idle, good-for-nothing beggars, and the sooner our streets are cleared of them, the better it will be for decent, hard-working, law-abiding subjects of the King. Go to work, I say. Go to church and pray for your souls. Glory be to the Father and to the Son and to the Holy Ghost. Amen.'

Wedderburn imitated Waddington's holy tone with sarcasm: 'Glory be to the Father and to the Son and to the Holy Ghost! The mother ought not to have been omitted in this family of idols. Glory be to the Father, to the Mother and to the Son would have sounded much better, even if Brothers and Sisters, Grandfather, Grandmama and Cousins had been omitted. I say to you that Christ was a Unitarian and a true Deist. And God is a very notorious Leveller.'

There were cheers, but this insult was too much for one Methodist in the congregation, who shouted: 'Damnable levelling doctrines. That's the foulest and most horrible blasphemy. You're an evil disposed and wicked person.'

Wedderburn turned on him quickly: 'What says our pious creature? The Methodist, whilst thumping his cushion, calls loudly for the curses of God on all Catholics, Unitarians and Deists. He tells his ignorant hearers that his is the true soul-saving shop, and that they will be damned, nay, double-damned, if they do not believe him.'

The Methodist replied earnestly: 'Methodists also wish to reform the country, but within the law of the land.'

Wedderburn resumed his speech:

I do not allow that any Methodist, or any bigot, deserves the epithet of a Reformer. He is mentally corrupt and ought first to reform himself. John Wesley was a friend to the King and urged his followers not to defraud his majesty of his just dues. We know what his majesty's just dues are! What did the Methodist Conference say just before the inhuman butcheries at Manchester? 'Fear God and honour the King. Meddle not with men who are given to change. Avoid tumultuous assemblies and wild delusive theories which are calculated to bring all government into contempt and to introduce universal discontent, insubordination and anarchy.'

How can these Methodists preach passive obedience to slaves in Jamaica, and support the Government's oppression here in England, and call themselves reformers? They cast out of their community all persons friendly to reform. The pulpits of the Methodists, like those of the Establishment, have for some time past rung with the doctrines of passive obedience and non-resistance. You must be as blind as a beetle. Your Conference issues bulls against the reformers. They issue fulminations against the cheap publications and against public meetings.

What can they see dangerous in the reform of the House of Commons?

The humility which was the character of the first Methodists is now nowhere to be seen. The priests of this sect, instead of riding about the country on a poor palfrey, with an allowance of sixpence per meal, are now splendidly accommodated in parsonage houses, and feel themselves as capable of bargaining with the Government of the day for the support of their whole sect, as ever the priests of the established church have done.

'Come now, and let us reason together.' Isaiah chapter 1, verse 18. We need not pin our faith upon the vain jangling of a pimp of a parson who neither practises nor believes what he puts upon the chuckle-headed fools he preaches to. God gave us reason to make use of for our present and future happiness, and whatever is contrary to it must be false.

Let us examine the Bible and see what absurdities it contains. Jesus Christ said no man had ever seen God. Then what a damned old liar Moses must have been, for he tells us he could run about and see God in every bush! Christ says no man ever conversed with God and yet that whoremonger Moses had a long conversation with him. Thus one or the other must be liars. Then there is Balaam's ass, oh yes, that spoke, and they tell us God put the words into his mouth. So I suppose God got into the jackass.

> *Should we not laugh that have a cause?*
> *Laughing does not invade the laws.*

Then there's the pretty story they tell us about the witch of Endor. Saul, who had been destroying all the witches as devils or what not, at last sends for the witch of Endor to raise up old Samuel to tell him what he was to do. Now Jesus Christ tells us that no one can raise the dead but God, so the witch must have the power of God.

Jesus Christ by the New Testament taught the Christian religion, but as religion is part and parcel of the law of the land, your fat-gutted parsons, priests or bishops would see Jesus Christ damned, or even God Almighty himself, rather than give up their twenty or thirty thousand a year and become pure curates at twenty pounds per annum. But what did he teach us? What did he say? Acknowledge no king; he was a reformer. Now every king is a lord, so he meant acknowledge no lord. Jesus Christ says acknowledge no rabbi, no priest. No, he knew their tricks and he says stand it no longer. Then Jesus Christ says acknowledge no fathers. Why? Because fathers in those days were allowed to thrash their sons at any age, the same as is allowed in Russia even to the present day.

Black preacher addressing slaves

Times were bad then and Christ became a radical reformer. Now I could never find out where he got his knowledge from, but this much I know from the same Book, that he was born of very poor parents, who like us felt with him the same as we now feel. And Christianity consists of what I've told you: acknowledge no king, acknowledge no priest, acknowledge no father. But this, my friends of liberty, was never practised. For that stupid fellow Paul, his apostle, that he left behind him, taught quite a different thing. He says pay your tribute money, pay Caesar, just like the Methodists tell us. But why did he say this? Why, because he knew his master had lost his life for saying otherwise. So, thought Paul, I'll tell them to pay their taxes, and then I may go and preach where I like, without being afraid of spies such as Oliver or Reynolds, or such as perhaps are now in this room, for Jesus Christ was betrayed by a spy. And so you see, there never was such a thing as Christianity ever practised in the world, least of all by Methodist missionaries in Jamaica.

The conclusion to Wedderburn's speech was greeted by cheers and clapping. Davenport jumped to his feet and shouted: 'Those in favour of the resolution.' All the hands shot up, except those of the Methodist and the spies. Davenport continued: 'I declare it carried overwhelmingly. Now I would like to propose a toast to Mr Carlile, spokesman for all mankind, white or black, red or brown, the Asian, the African, the European and the American. And may we live to see the day when the heads of five wicked priests shall be sold for a penny. May the last of the kings be strangled with the guts of the last of the priests. Citizens, let us drink the health of all those who have been and are now engaged in the cause of human liberty:

> *What is it that props the chair of state?*
> *What shields the wasteful tyrant's throne?*
> *What fills the clergy's purse and plate?*
> *What gives deceit its specious tone?*
> *What makes the senseless millions slaves?*
> *What forged the chains of mean condition?*
> *What spread dread terror round men's graves?*
> *What fools the mind? – BASE SUPERSTITION!!*

Then Wedderburn rose to propose a toast: 'To the bulwark of justice, trial by jury, and may the cowardly machinations of tyranny ever be defeated by the courage of honest jurors! I give you Tommy Spence and the People's Farm.' Davenport continued the toast in verse:

> *That man, that honest man, old Tommy Spence,*
> *Whose genius, judgement, wit, and common sense,*
> *Confounded all the dogmas of the schools,*
> *And prov'd that statesmen are but learned fools,*
> *That priests preach future worlds of pain and bliss*
> *To cheat the weak and rob the poor in this!*
> *Or else their practice and their cry would be,*
> *'Let all be equal and let all be free!'*

The last line was repeated by the congregation as a chant and then Billy Waters concluded the proceedings by singing a song to the tune of the Lass of Richmond Hill, with everyone joining in the chorus:

> *Ye maidens fair and matrons kind,*
> *Come listen unto me,*
> *While I relate the joys we'll find*
> *On Spence's Jubilee.*
> *This Jubilee when all are free,*
> *We'll dance the roundalay,*
> *With music sweet, the morn we'll greet,*
> *Of that great happy day.*

It is our right to have and hold
The Land on which we dwell,
And share the rents as Spence has told,
Land none may buy or sell.
    This Jubilee etc.

Dame nature did this right bestow
When first the world began;
Can landlords better titles show,
'Tis the whole rights of man.
    This Jubilee etc.

Come lend your aid ye lovely fair,
Assistance give it free;
Then opposition who will dare,
When sexes both agree.
    With trumpet's sound, the Land around,
    Call forth each Family,
    To take the rent the quarter's spent,
    This is the Jubilee

This reign of plenty, peace and love,
The good have long foretold;
A bless'd millennium will prove
To mankind young and old.
    No more distress, all happiness,
    From Landlords once set free,
    The bells shall ring, we'll dance and sing,
    On Spence's Jubilee.

CHAPTER SIX

WEDDERBURN'S TRIAL AND IMPRISONMENT, 1820

Although Wedderburn was acquitted for sedition, it was not long before he was re-arrested on a charge of blasphemy. He was committed to Newgate Jail, for want of bail, and on Friday 25 February 1820 his trial took place before the Lord Chief Justice and a special jury in the court of the King's Bench, Westminster.

The Solicitor-General introduced the case: 'My Lord, the defendant used blasphemous language with intent to excite impiety and irreligion in the minds of his majesty's subjects, and to vilify the Christian religion. This blasphemous language was uttered in a place called Hopkins Street Chapel, near Berwick Street, in Soho. The place had been for some time used for debating on political and religious subjects, and, from the extraordinary freedom with which every topic was handled, it had attracted the attention of the magistrates, who thought it necessary to send some person on whom they could rely to notice what was passing.' He then called on William Plush as a witness and asked him if he knew where these debates were held.

'I do,' replied Plush. 'It is called Hopkins Street Chapel, though it's really only a hayloft. I was directed to go there last year and observe the defendant.' The Solicitor-General nodded and waited for Plush to continue. Plush began to read:

The subject announced for consideration on the evening in question was 'Whether the refusal of the Chief-Justice to allow Mr Carlile to read the bible in his defence was to be attributed to the sincere respect he had for the sacred writings, or to a fear lest the absurdities it contained should be exposed?'

After complimenting the two previous speakers the defendant begged leave to call their attention to a few absurdities they had not noticed. He then said: 'Christianity, it is true, has been introduced, but it has never been followed. Judge Abbot has no doubt read the bible and knows pretty well the absurdities it contains.'

Plush went on to give a fairly accurate description of Wedderburn's speech that night when he ridiculed Moses and the burning bush, and criticized the corruption of the clergy. Wedderburn was amazed at the detail his statement contained and asked him, 'Did you commit this account of what I said to writing?'

'I did, part in the evening and part the next morning.'

'Of what religion are you?' asked Wedderburn

'Of the Christian religion and bred in the principles of the Church of England, so I know what blasphemy is.'

'What is your profession?'

'I am a parish constable,' replied Plush

The Solicitor-General then called as a witness Matthew Matthewson, who said, 'I accompanied Mr Plush to Hopkins Street and agree with his report. I wrote down as much as I could remember that evening and when I met Mr Plush the next morning we arranged the thing together.'

The Lord Chief Justice intervened: 'How did you arrange it together?'

'He told me what he remembered of the blasphemy and I would not allow him to put down anything that I did not recollect. I was employed to go to the meeting. I am a journeyman tailor by profession. I have received nothing for my trouble, but I expect to be remunerated for the loss of time.'

The Lord Chief Justice ignored this remark and called the defendant, who rose and addressed the court in measured tones:

*Gentlemen of the jury, I am the offspring of a female slave, by a rich European planter. My **Christian** father sold my mother while pregnant with me, in consequence of which I have received no education. Being fascinated with the reports of Christianity, I thought, when at home in Jamaica, that if I could once get to a Christian country, I should be happy; but on my arrival here, I found the number of sects so great, that my mind was distracted with doubts raised by the various conflicting opinions which were entertained by them. I first mixed with the Arminians, then with the Calvinists, and afterwards fell into the Unitarian persuasion. Being capable by argument to overcome any Arminian or Calvinist, I consequently concluded my present doctrines to be the most rational.*

As it is very natural for persons wishing to promulgate what they think is true, in opposition to what they consider erroneous, I opened a chapel. Finding that although people were punished with death two hundred years ago for denying the trinity, yet that now the King, by and with the consent of the lords spiritual and temporal and privy council, has granted us permission to deny the trinity and to preach many doctrines without fear, which were heretofore prohibited as blasphemy, I procured myself to be licensed as a Unitarian preacher and certainly had no suspicion of being called to account for what I am now charged with.

By trade I am a journeyman tailor and my sight now is very poor. I am under the necessity of making my own defence for two reasons, first, because I am so poor that I cannot afford fee counsel; and secondly, because if a barrister would plead my cause gratuitously, he would not dare to do it upon principle.

Your minds are endeavoured to be prejudiced against me, by the frequent repetition of the term 'blasphemy'; but what, after all, is the meaning of this word, so terrific in the ears of the ignorant and superstitious? It simply means to defame or slander. Now, if I utter anything against a public or private individual of my own species, their persons and character are known, and it can be ascertained whether what I have said be true or false. But how can I be said to slander, defame, or blast, or blacken the reputation of the Deity, when your very religion itself teaches you that he is incomprehensible, that no one has ever seen or conversed with him, that we are finite beings and that he is infinite. How then is it possible, seeing we cannot know or comprehend this infinite being, that we can say aught against him, or that our finite nature can injure one who is represented as omnipotent and omniscient? But independent of this mode of reasoning, I defy the most inveterate of my enemies that can be found among the innumerable fanatics of the day, to prove that I have ever written, or spoken, a single word derogatory to the honour of the Deity.

There is no one will deny the value and importance of truth, but how is it to be ascertained, if we are not allowed the liberty of free inquiry? Does not Paul tell us to 'prove all things and to hold fast to the best'; but how are we to be determined in our choice, if we are not allowed to canvass and discuss the merits or demerits of particular systems? And as for the right of private judgement, it is fully established by Christ himself, where he says: 'Why judge ye not for yourselves that which is right?' After this, what man professing to respect the religion of Jesus can defend persecution on the ground of a difference in opinion? Every person of common sense must see that it is the same spirit which now persecutes me, that brought the founder of Christianity to the cross.

I am aware that I shall be told, the state religion is not set up as a golden image which I am compelled to worship; but that whatever may be my ideas against it, I must not utter them, lest by possibility they should be construed into ridicule and reviling. How weak one would think must be that cause which is afraid of allowing you to laugh. They say we may discuss theological subjects coolly, seriously and learnedly; but that we must not treat them with levity or sarcasm. Do they act up to the maxim of Christ? Do they do as they would be done by? Do they not, on the contrary, take the liberty to ridicule all the solemn forms, rites, ceremonies and observances of the Catholic church, and call it superstition, mummery, pantomime, scarlet whore of Babylon etc? Do they not call Mahomet an impostor, and his religion a cheat? And yet they have the gravity and assurance to forbid the same freedoms being taken with themselves.

I cannot but blush at the weakness and bad policy of those who seek to support their cause by the persecution of a humble individual like myself, when the clergymen of the established church of England alone are 20,000, and their wages amount to two millions annually. In addition to these, there are 50,000 dissenting ministers of different denominations; then, there are bible societies, religious tract societies, and institutions for the promotion of Christian knowledge in every part of the country. Yet all this redoubtable phalanx are not sufficient to defend Christianity, without resorting to the arm of power.

Is not this itself a far greater libel on their religion than anything I have said? Is it not stated that the gates of hell shall not prevail against it? If they are sincere in their belief, that its origin is divine, why fear the efforts of a mortal man? If they cannot protect it by fair means, they should not degrade it be resorting to such unworthy measures. They should pretend to treat me with contempt, and say I was beneath their notice; that I was a poor deluded enthusiast.

Before I go into a vindication of the alleged libel, it is essentially necessary you should know the precise manner in which it occurred. It was my custom to open my chapel on two evenings during the week for conferences on theological subjects and to discuss such questions as were proposed by the members of my church. On the night charged in the indictment I felt it my duty to prove that there were both absurdities and falsehoods in the bible. And where, after all, is my crime? It consists merely in having spoken in the same plain and homely language which Christ and his disciples uniformly used. If I had asserted the same things a thousand times in a different phraseology, no notice would have been taken, but because my audience were humble people who would not have understood fine-spun discourses and delicate allusions, I am to be condemned for addressing them in the vulgar tongue.

Indeed there seems to be a conspiracy against the poor, to keep them in ignorance and superstition. The rich may have as many copies as they like of such sceptical writers as Shaftesbury, Hume and Gibbon, because they are above the reach or comprehension of the lower orders, but if I find two most decided contradictions in the bible, I must not in the language of the same book assert that one or other is a lie. As I have far greater respect for Christ than for Moses, my bias is to believe the former when he asserted what was rational and probable, namely 'that no man hath seen God', in preference to the latter, who represented himself as having frequent interviews with the Deity, and 'speaking to him face to face, as a man speaketh to his friend'. Exodus chapter 33, verse 11.

And who will have the presumption to deny that the story of Saul and the witch of Endor is not an absurdity? It might have done very well for the time in which it was written, and even in this country at an earlier period, when the very judges themselves who sat in this court believed in witchcraft, and pronounced sentence of condemnation against unfortunate women, who were prosecuted for that supposed crime; but who is there now that has faith in such idle tales, or that can credit the power of a wizard or a witch to raise the prophet Samuel, or any other person, from the dead?

As to my explanation of the doctrines of Christ, I must still maintain it to be particularly faithful. He was, like myself, one of the lower order, and a genuine radical reformer. Being poor himself, he knew how to feel for the poor, and he despised the rich for the hardness of their hearts. His principles were purely republican: he told his followers they were all brethren and equals, and inculcated a thorough contempt for all the tithes, pomps and dignities of this world. He established no priesthood, but on the contrary he said to them: 'Be ye not called rabbi.' Matthew chapter 23, verse 8.

He was a mild and amiable man, whose object was to benefit the poor and oppressed, but being cut off in his career through spies and informers, his system was never properly established, and though his name has been made a cloak and stalking-horse for the worst purposes, his religion has never been followed. For my part, though I consider Jesus Christ to have been deceived in the application of some passages in the Jewish scriptures to himself, yet I have ever revered his principles and regretted they were never put in practice.

Gentlemen of the jury, it is customary for persons in my situation to flatter you and to say everything they can to court your verdict in their favour, but all I shall say is to remind you that, notwithstanding you are sworn on the evangelists, yet, being in this case the judge of both law and fact, you are fully competent to acquit me of having uttered a blasphemous libel. And I shall merely add that if there is among you but one man who thoroughly understands and respects the religion of Jesus, one sincere friend to religious liberty and the universal right of conscience, I shall be acquitted. But if, on the contrary, the spirit of bigotry and religious persecution prevails over you, I shall have this satisfaction, that I suffer like Christ and his disciples for boldly asserting what I deem to be true; and as nature has blest me with a calm and tranquil mind, I shall be far happier in the dungeon to which you may consign me than my persecutors on their beds of down.

As Wedderburn sat down, the Solicitor-General smiled superciliously and rose to address the court:

The defendant has produced no evidence to counteract or invalidate the evidence on the part of the prosecution. On the contrary, the defence he has put in has admitted and attempted to justify the charge which has been preferred against him. The defendant has complained much about the spirit of religious persecution, but surely, gentlemen of the jury, you must see that this prosecution does not arise from such a spirit. The defendant is at liberty to entertain what sentiments or follow what religion he pleases, but he must not bring into contempt the sacred scriptures and the Christian religion, as established by law in this country.

He says that his audience were of the lower order and therefore he was under the necessity of addressing them in a language suitable to their understandings. This is the very reason why the defendant ought to be prosecuted. A person professing the sentiments and possessing the popular talents of the defendant is particularly dangerous among the class of people to whom he has alluded. The magistrates would have been guilty of a dereliction of their duty if, knowing the nature of these debates, they had not attempted to put a stop to them. Far from being instigated by an uncharitable feeling, or from motives of persecution, the public officers are actuated solely by a solicitous attention to preserve the morals of the poor and to prevent their minds from being deprived of the necessary restraints of religion.

Can it be tolerated that a man like the defendant should thus set at defiance the laws of his country and turn into ridicule those writings which form the foundation of our holy religion, and upon which are built the hopes of all good men. I therefore trust that if you credit the testimony of the witnesses on the part of the crown, you will find the defendant guilty.

Satisfied that his logic was indisputable, the Solicitor-General sat down, and the Lord Chief Justice then summed up the case:

Gentlemen of the jury, the charge brought against the defendant has been most clearly proved by the evidence on the part of the prosecution. The defendant has produced no witnesses to contradict the statements made by those on the side of the crown; on the contrary, with some trifling exceptions, he seems to admit the truth of their evidence.

The only question in this case is, whether you believe the circumstances related by the two witnesses. If you do believe, from their testimony, that the words were spoken by the defendant, then you must find him guilty.

The defendant has put in a defence which I must acknowledge is exceedingly well drawn up; and the sentiments and reasoning, as far as applies to persecution on the ground of religion, are particularly just; but the defendant was not charged here with entertaining this or that opinion, but with openly reviling that religion which is identified with, and is the foundation of, justice in this country.

The jury will retire to consider their verdict.

The verdict was never in doubt. The jury discussed the matter for three quarters of an hour and then found Wedderburn guilty. They recommended mercy, however, because they considered him to have erred through ignorance and for want of care in his early years.

Two and a half months after the verdict, the court reconvened for the sentence. The Lord Chief Justice began by asking Wedderburn if he had any affidavits to present. Wedderburn replied:

No, but I have something further to say. In consequence of being thrown into prison, my chapel has been shut up and my congregation dispersed. These circumstances have prevented me from seeking from amongst them evidence to contradict or invalidate the testimony on the part of the crown. My memory is extremely bad and it is impossible for me to recollect all I might have said on that occasion. Every observation I made arose spontaneously on the spur of the moment. My sermons or speeches were never the result of previous contrivance, but I certainly remember to have spoken upon the story of the Witch of Endor.

My impression on this subject arose from having seen my aged grandmother, a poor black slave in the island of Jamaica, several times most cruelly flogged by order of her master, a white man and a Christian, for being a witch. Now, when I was a child, I frequently picked her pocket of sixpences and shillings, so I was well convinced she could not possess the powers attributed to witches, or she must surely have detected my petty theft. When I became a Christian and read the story of Saul and the Witch of Endor, with these impressions upon my mind, I could never bring myself to believe that such characters could work miracles and raise the dead.

I also remember telling the story in the bible about God speaking out of the mouth of Balaam's ass, God becoming a donkey, and mentioning that whoremonger Moses and that bloody murderer David, and what about that liar and fool Joshua, commanding the sun to stand still...

The shocked gasps of outrage from people in the court led the Lord Chief Justice to intervene: 'No, no, we can't tolerate language of such a nature in this court!' But Wedderburn persisted more politely:

May it please your Lordship, however humble I may be as a member of society, and whatever efforts may be made to degrade me and render me contemptible in the eyes of the world, I have nevertheless the pride, and the ambition, to flatter myself that even my simple exertions will one day or other be of no mean importance to the cause I am embarked in, which is that of Religious Liberty and the Universal Right of Conscience.

If we would obtain the privileges to which we are entitled, neither death nor dungeons must terrify us; we must keep in mind the example of Christ and his apostles. I feel persuaded that no effort, however humble, will ultimately be lost to the cause of Truth and Liberty; and that even my trifling productions may, perhaps, 'like bread cast on the waters, be seen after many days'. It is by slow degrees that all new truths are propagated, because they must necessarily meet with considerable opposition from the ignorant, the prejudiced, and above all from those whose interests would be injured by the public adoption of these new truths.

We have not to thank any human being for our right to think, as 'tis neither in their power, nor our own, to control our thoughts. Neither chains, nor dungeons, nor the terrors of being burnt alive, can prevent us from thinking freely. Neither ought they to prevent us from speaking freely, writing freely, and publishing freely, if we think we can benefit mankind by exposing falsehood and error.

Those doctrines which would have been confined to my obscure chapel, to my small congregation, are now, by the fostering aid of my prosecutors, published to the whole world. They have effectually advertised the very thing which they dislike. By preventing me from preaching, they have compelled me to become an author. They have dragged me from obscurity into public notice and made me a member of the Republic of Letters.

My prosecutors evince great ignorance of human nature, if they think they can tell the world of the existence of a singular doctrine, or a curious book, without at the same time creating in them a strong desire to become acquainted with it. They should keep in mind the story of our great grandmother Eve and the tree of knowledge. She was forbidden to taste its fruit, lest her eyes should be opened, but her curiosity could not resist the temptation to disobey, though the punishment attached was so great.

I know I shall be told again that 'tis not my doctrines, but my language, for which I am prosecuted. This I contend is contemptible sophistry. If I am a low, vulgar man, and incapable of delivering my sentiments in an elegant and polished manner, am I to be condemned, when I find two pages in the Bible most palpably contradicting each other, for asserting that one of them must be a lie? For stating the history of the Witch of Endor to be an idle tale and old woman's story? For attempting to divest the simple republican system of Jesus of those gaudy appendages, those trumpery additions, with which craft and ignorance combined have conspired to corrupt its native purity, its original simplicity? If this is not permitted, if any system is to be considered infallible, a bar is put to all human improvement.

I have no fear that the remaining liberties of this country can be destroyed as long as there are people willing to suffer, and I am proud in reflecting that there are hundreds like myself who aspire to the crown of martyrdom.

My Lord, some persons in my situation would endeavour to press upon your consideration the jury's recommendation to mercy and the long imprisonment I experienced before I was bailed out to prepare my defence. But it is by no means my wish to obtrude these circumstances on the notice of your Lordship, as I am so extremely poor that a prison will be a home to me. As I am so far advanced in life, I shall esteem it an honour to die immured in a dungeon for advocating the cause of truth, of religious liberty, and the universal right of conscience.

The Solicitor-General was not impressed by Wedderburn's arguments, but recognized his skill as an orator. He also realized that Wedderburn's attack on orthodox religion implied an attack on established political authority as well. He addressed the court:

As you can see, the defendant is a most dangerous character because he certainly possesses considerable talents, and those too of a popular nature, and calculated to do much mischief amongst the class of people to whom he is in the habit of addressing himself. It must be recollected that his place of holding forth is a licensed chapel, and he himself a licensed preacher of the Unitarian persuasion. All these circumstances form a protection for him and he has made use of this for the purpose of undermining and reviling the religion of the country.

This notorious firebrand complains that the prosecution is the result of a persecuting spirit of religious bigotry, but we can assure him it is not on the score of his opinions, however offensive, but for the open, scurrilous, gross and violent manner in which he has attacked, scandalized and reviled the Christian religion. If he had but delivered his sentiments in a cautious, decent and guarded manner, this prosecution would never have been instituted, but such language as his, addressed to the lower orders of the community, can never be tolerated.

The Lord Chief Justice was in total agreement and was just as keen to protect the authority of the Bible and its role in upholding the authority of the state. He was not impressed with Wedderburn's unapologetic stance and considered him an enemy of society:

You have been convicted by a jury of making use, in a certain discourse, of the blasphemous and profane words which have been detailed in the evidence, language calculated to distress the feelings of those who entertain a reverence for the sacred scriptures. It cannot be tolerated. It does not show ignorance, but, I am sorry to say, a perverted and depraved talent.

The book you so impiously revile is of great antiquity and contains not only the religion of this country, but of many others, and of all civilised and enlightened nations. It has received the sanction of ages, it is the foundation of all courts of justice, and consequently, whenever it has received any violent attack, this court has always shown the offenders that it was a great crime, and punished them accordingly.

The Christian religion wants not the arm of man or of the law to support it, but it is nevertheless the duty of those who have to protect the public tranquillity, to prevent all attempts to destroy it. Those who have leisure to investigate its internal evidence cannot be injured by such doctrines as yours, for I am convinced no one can be an infidel who will examine it with candour and impartiality. It contains nothing but good will towards man. It is calculated to render him more humble, more submissive, and in every way a better member of society, and of course to advance the happiness of mankind.

Those persons who have an opportunity of calmly examining it want no protection, but there are a vast many who have ears to hear, but not leisure to study and reflect, and it is for their protection that this prosecution is instituted.

This is a country of great freedom, but that freedom must not be suffered to launch into licentiousness. I regret, from the nature of what you offer, that the same disposition of hostility towards religion, which animated you when you committed the offence, still appears to influence your conduct.

When persons stand upon the floor of this court to answer for an offence, it is possible they may diminish the quantum of punishment by proving that they have repented of their crime, but you still persist in justifying it, which is an aggravation of your offence. You are an enemy at the heart of the state. It is our duty then to remove you, at least for a time, from society, that you may be prevented doing it a further injury by the dissemination of your dangerous doctrines.

The Court do therefore sentence you to be imprisoned for two years in his majesty's jail at Dorchester, and, at the expiration of that time, to enter into sureties, yourself in £50 and two other persons £25 each, for your good behaviour for three years more.

DORCHESTER JAIL

> **I'll not forget thee, noble man!**
> **Tho' a dungeon's darkness hide thee,**
> **Disgrace thee never tyrants can,**
> **I'll bless thee more, the more they chide thee.**

This was not the last that the Lord Chief Justice was to hear of Robert Wedderburn, for in the spring of 1820, when the five men of Cato Street were being hanged at Newgate, Elizabeth Wedderburn decided to send him a letter complaining about her husband's imprisonment in Dorchester. With the help of George Cannon, her husband's friend and fellow Spencean, she wrote:

To the Lord Chief Justice. My Lord, to send a rich man to a distant jail is not so great a punishment as to send a poor man to the same place, because a rich man can have every luxury but liberty. When a poor man is imprisoned, it ought to be where his family and friends can reach him to throw in a morsel of victuals through the bars of his dungeon.

If you had imprisoned Mr Wedderburn in Newgate, he would then have had a small portion of meat, according to the jail allowance, and his family could have divided their own scanty meals to make him up sufficient to support nature. But by sending him to a distant jail, 150 miles away, where no meat is allowed, and beyond the reach of his distressed family, the punishment is just double to him, to what it would be to another person. And you well know, my Lord, that the parish to which he belongs will make no allowance, even if the man should die by starvation.

Mr Wedderburn is a poor journeyman tailor, on the verge of 60, and I am too poor to render him any assistance.

I have heard that you are the most humane of all the judges and I hope that, when approaching the throne of Grace to supplicate mercy for yourself, you will remember that a poor religious enthusiast, as pious and sincere in his way as you are in yours, is thrust into a solitary dungeon for two years. There he has to live upon grey pease and barley broth, merely because he differed in opinion from the state religion, and had too much honesty, and too little education, to wrap his sentiments up in that 'cautious, decent, and guarded manner' which the Solicitor-General said he could tolerate.

I am your Lordship's most obedient servant, Elizabeth Wedderburn.

Needless to say, the Lord Chief Justice was sure enough of his welcome at the throne of Grace that he did not feel the need to respond.

Another prisoner at Dorchester Jail at this time was the famous radical journalist and printer Richard Carlile. In October 1819 he had been found guilty of blasphemous libel, fined £1500 and sentenced to three years imprisonment. His wife Jane continued to run his bookshop in Fleet Street, but in the following year she too was arrested for selling Sherwin's *Life of Paine* and her husband's weekly paper *The Republican*. She was banned from selling books and then sent to join her husband in Dorchester Jail. Carlile's sister, Mary Ann, then took over the running of the shop and Carlile continued to produce his paper from prison.

Carlile, who came from Devonshire, was only half Wedderburn's age, but he was wealthy enough to enjoy much better conditions in prison. His cell was light and airy with a sink, bed, desk, some furniture, and weights to keep him fit. He was in the habit of trying out his editorials on his wife: 'The Christian religion has been called the religion of peace, but where shall we look for the practical part of that assertion? In the persecution of booksellers? Shall we look into Dorchester Jail for it, and see a whole family immured for calling it in question, and for wishing to have it examined? Where, where is the peace among Christians? When, when was it, or when shall it be? Let it begin now, gentlemen. Discountenance this persecution. Tolerate the opinions which may differ from yours and you shall find peace. There will be no peace until you do so, and experience teaches us that every persecuted opinion destroys its persecutors. Jane has the laundry gone yet?'

'No, m'dear.'

'Can you call him, then?'

'Yes, m'dear.'

Jane went to the cell door and knocked. Carlile carried on reading: 'A priest is a priest all the world over. It matters not to what religion he ministers, there is an universal sameness in their motives: to live in splendour and luxury without performing any productive labour, to demand the homage and even the worship of the labouring and cheated multitude!'

The turnkey came to the cell door and asked gruffly: 'What is it?'

Jane replied, 'The laundry.'

Carlile asked her, 'Have you put my night-cap in the bag?'

'It's on your head, m'dear.'

Carlile took it off and gave it to the turnkey: 'Right, there you are. And can you take this to the printer. It should just about make it in time for the next issue. We also could do with some more coal and I need some more paper.' He gave the man some money.

'Thank you, sir.'

Carlile picked up the weights and started exercising: 'Who was that just admitted?'

'A man called Wedderburn.'

'Wedderburn!'

'Yes, sir. He say he's going to spend his time here learning to write.'

'I thought he already could. I've read some of his pamphlets.'

'He says he dictates what he wants written and then a friend writes it down.'

Carlile smiled: 'I could get him appointed as prison chaplain! Which cell is he in?'

'The one next to yours.'

'Not that dingy hole. It's so dark and damp, and there's not enough room to swing a cat!'

'Yes, sir. He got to stay in solitary confinement for two years. No privileges, nothing.'

'Can I speak to him?' Carlile offered the turnkey some more money.

'No, that's more 'n my life's worth. He bain't be allowed to speak to nobody.'

'Well, will you ask him if he wants any books, paper or money?'

'I'll see.'

'And here's some fruit for him. And ask him if he wants any money for coal. It's freezing in that cell.'

'I'm afraid to take him money, sir.'

'My God, what are they trying to do to him? What is this spirit that prosecutes him? The spirit of bigotry, of tyranny, of revenge. All he's done is point out the contradictions in the bible. He's an old man. If his health is destroyed or death hastened, I shall not hesitate a moment to charge you with participating in his murder. We have already had one death in the prison. The present system of jail discipline is nothing but a system of revenge, torture and mental degradation. The Governor is an insensate machine!'

'Yes, sir. I have some post for you, sir.'

Carlile, who had been exercising all this time, put down the weights and opened one of the letters. 'Jane, it's from my sister, Mary Ann.'

'How is she?'

'She's been arrested and convicted... and they're sending her here! How will we manage?'

'We'll manage.' Jane stuck out her stomach and stretched her arms. 'There'll soon be four of us, then!'

Carlile grimaced and then opened the other letter. 'This one contains £1 collected for Rev Wedderburn.' He turned to the turnkey. 'Can you at least give him this?'

'No, sir. The magistrates' rules are that it must first be sent to the post office in Dorchester. I must submit it in a letter to the Governor who will then give it to me to take to the post office in Dorchester. I must then call again at the post office and bring it back to the Governor who will then forward it to Mr Wedderburn.'

'And what about my receipt?'

'The rules are that Mr Wedderburn must send his receipt to the Governor who will give it to me to take to the post office. Then I must call for it again and bring it back to the Governor, who will give it to me to give to you.' The turnkey was very pleased to have enunciated the procedure correctly.

Carlile was not so pleased. 'My God, and this is meant to be a reformed prison! The imbecility is scandalous.'

'Yes, sir. Be that all, sir?'

'Yes. Come back later for our walk. Wait, has that canting prison visitor Wilberforce been seen here lately?'

'He'm due to come today, sir, to see the new prisoner. I'm expecting him at any moment.'

'God help him! Do you remember, Jane, when Wilberforce organized that dinner to celebrate the international outlawing of the slave trade? He invited negroes from the streets of London, but insisted that they were separated from him and the other guests by a screen set across one end of the room. The old hypocrite!'

Carlile sat down and started writing again, reading out what he was writing: 'Our duty is to employ ourselves in undermining the hideous structure now existing, and the moment we have accomplished this first necessary object, then to begin to discuss the best plan for the new structure. To be quarrelling about the new plan, and to leave the old rubbish to remove itself, is not wisdom, in my judgement...'

WILBERFORCE VISITS WEDDERBURN

Meanwhile, down the corridor in an altogether different type of cell sat Robert Wedderburn on a wooden bench. The room measured thirty foot by six foot. It was dank and dark, with water dripping down the walls. There was the sound of a key turning in the lock. The turnkey entered and announced: 'There be a visitor for you.'

To Wedderburn's surprise, he ushered in a man disguised with a long beard who obviously had poor eyesight. He stumbled in the gloom and then sat down next to Wedderburn.

'Who are you?'

'I have come to talk to you about the love of Christ, how he can forgive your sins and save your soul from damnation. We are a nation, which besides the invaluable benefit of an unequalled degree of true civil liberty, has been favoured with an unprecedented measure of religious light, with its long train of attendant blessings.'

Wedderburn was taken aback. It wasn't the language he was used to, unless it was part of the bombastic theatricals of Hopkins Street Chapel. But he managed to ask bitterly, 'What civil liberty is there here?'

'Your body may be in prison but your soul can be made free. I have seen how Christianity cheers the hearts and elevates the principles, and dignifies the conduct of multitudes of our labouring classes in this free and enlightened country.'

'Multitudes of our labouring classes are starving to death! Where's the dignity in that?'

'But the lower classes are the preferable objects of the love of the Almighty.'

William Wilberforce

'What evidence is there of that?'

'The present life is but a short and uncertain span, to which will succeed an eternal existence of happiness for those who repent and seek forgiveness. The Lord's my shepherd, I'll not want.'

'Why then does he tolerate the condition of slavery?'

'We are His instruments on earth to do his will. Our ultimate success is sure; and ere long we shall rejoice in the consciousness of having delivered our country from the greatest of her crimes, and rescued her character from the deepest stain of dishonour. Our African brethren shall soon be free. For two hundred years they have been kept in pagan darkness and depravity, without any religious instruction. Promiscuous intercourse between the sexes and pagan darkness are nearly universal among them. They are strangers to the institution of marriage. But now we are bringing them into the blessed light of Christianity. No sooner does a Negro become a Christian, than the Obeah-man despairs of bringing him into subjection.'

'Are they not both alike, Obeah and Christianity? Base superstition.'

'God forbid.'

'My grandmother used to tell me a story about Woss-Woss. She knew that one day we would be free. But how long will it take to set my people free?'

'The slaves may not yet be fit for the enjoyment of British freedom. They must be prepared for the enjoyment of civil rights. But the time will soon come when a degraded slave population will be turned into a free and industrious peasantry.'

'Like the free and industrious peasantry of England, you mean!'

'I have heard that argument before. Many West Indian planters say that their Negro slaves are as well or even better off than our British peasantry. It is a monstrous proposition to compare the state of a West Indian slave with that of an English freeman and to give the former preference.'

'The slaves will free themselves, just as they did in San Domingo. You have not heard the last of revolution in Jamaica.'

'Those dreadful incidents of San Domingo. That is not the way to freedom.'

'Is it for you to decide how we win our freedom?'

Wilberforce held up the bible he was clutching. 'You must study the word of God.'

'I wish to have nothing to do with that book; and you cannot wonder at this, for if that book be true, I am damned for ever!'

'No, no, Mr Wedderburn. According to this book, there is hope for all who will seek for mercy and forgiveness, for it assures us that God hath no pleasure in the death of him that dieth.'

'How can you call that the word of God? Those obscene stories, cruel and tortuous executions, the unrelenting vindictiveness. More like the word of a demon than the word of God. Does not the Bible tell us that the assassination of infants was done by the express command of God? To believe the Bible to be true, we must unbelieve all our belief in the moral justice of God.'

'But the new testament tells of God's love in sending Jesus Christ to atone for our sins.'

'He that believes in the story of Christ is an infidel to God. The story of Mary and Joseph, taken as it is told, is blasphemously obscene. It gives an account of a young woman engaged to be married, and while under this engagement she is, to speak in plain language, debauched by a ghost.'

Wilberforce was horrified and becoming more and more

uncomfortable, both physically, because of the hard bench he was sitting on, and psychologically because of the attack on his religion. He tried to stay calm. 'But the church gives guidance on how to interpret the scriptures.'

Wedderburn felt as if he were back in Hopkins Street Chapel addressing the citizens. 'All churches appear to me no other than human inventions, set up to terrify and enslave mankind, and monopolize power and profit. The most detestable wickedness, the most horrid cruelties and the greatest miseries that have afflicted the human race, have had their origin in religion.'

'Do you not believe in the Bible at all?'

'The creation is the Bible of the Deist.'

Wilberforce changed tack. 'I know you are an honest and conscientious man.'

Wedderburn was becoming tired of his condescending tone and wanted the meeting to be over. 'I am a worn out flint tailor, striving to immortalize my fame in the cause of humanity, regardless of death or imprisonment, which ought to be the sentiment of every individual who is deprived of his just right. I should have gone back to Jamaica, had I not been fearful of the planters; for such is their hatred of anyone having black blood in his veins, and who dares to think and act as a free man, that they would most certainly have trumped up some charge against me, and hung me.'

Wilberforce thought he had done his duty. 'My friend, I will leave you now, but please take these two books for your consolation. I hope to return shortly.'

'Thank you. God send us better days; we cannot have worse.'

'I wish you good evening.' He got up and knocked on the cell door.

'Good evening,' replied Wedderburn as the jailer let Wilberforce out.

WEDDERBURN'S DREAM

Wedderburn was weary. He lay on his wooden bed and opened one of the books he had been given. Soon, however, his eyes closed and the book slipped from his hands.

He heard a noise which at first sounded like keys clanking on a chain, but the clicking and whirring gradually got louder and louder and a series of huge clockwork figures entered his cell, one by one. They were clearly machines, but were dressed in clothes that immediately identified them.

First came a ten-feet-high replica of the Prince Regent, now King George IV. There followed in the procession Aristocracy preceded by his fat belly, Lord Castlereagh with a razor hanging round his neck, Lord Sidmouth pulling a crocodile behind him, William Wilberforce, a Methodist Preacher dressed in black, the Archbishop of Canterbury carrying a huge bible, James Wedderburn and the Lord Chief Justice.

They seemed to be moving smoothly forward of their own volition, but then it became clear that underneath their trousers or cassocks were people pushing the great machines along on wheels. The figures surrounded Wedderburn and then came to a stop, all of them pointing metal fingers at him. Then out stepped Waddington, to be followed by Allen Davenport, Billy Waters, Joseph Johnson, Ephraim, Moses, Dusty Bob, Elizabeth Wedderburn and William Davidson. They stood formally in front of their respective clockwork characters.

Waddington was the first to move. He jumped up on a stool and addressed the bemused Wedderburn: 'O true and infallible genius of prophetic skill, Hopkins Street Chapel is closed. The light has gone out. The laughter has evaporated in the night air. The Prince Regent, who is now King George IV, Squire Whelps, resides in his palace, a cold fish. He has not long to live.'

Davenport opened his book of poems, but then looked up and recited by heart:

> *The field inclos'd is common field no more;*
> *So pass away the comforts of the poor!*
> *When labour fails, as at the present time,*
> *What can succeed but poverty and crime!*

'Aristocracy still struts about the land, but not for long. His days are numbered.'

> *Tremble, O tyrants of the world*
> *And you, O fallen slaves, arise.*

'What is sown in this generation, if not reaped by ourselves, will produce an ample harvest in the next generation.'

Waters, with his parrot on his shoulder, followed with a song:

> *God rest you, merry Gentlemen,*
> *Let nothing you dismay.*

> *Remember we were left alive*
> *Upon last Christmas day,*
> *With both our lips at liberty*
> *To praise Lord Castlereagh*
> *With his 'practical' comfort and joy!*

He added triumphantly, 'Lord Sidmouth has resigned!'

'And Lord Castlereagh will cut his own throat,' screamed Joseph Johnson. 'Let that sound reach you in the depth of your dungeon and let it carry consolation to your suffering soul. I shall sing again.'

Ephraim said firmly, 'Comrade, I now see Wilberforce for the canting hypocrite he is. He will not set us free. We can only free ourselves. Freedom is to be won, not granted.'

Moses reached out his staff and proclaimed, 'Brother, as Moses delivered the Israelites out of the house of bondage, so will we fight for our freedom. No Methodist preacher will prevent us. The Lord has surely seen the affliction of our people and has heard our cry by reason of our taskmasters. He surely knows our sorrows. Jamaica will soon be in revolt again.'

Dusty Bob stepped forward with his white stick and his dog Jeremiah: 'The Archbishop still lives in his grand palace. He passed me the other day and threw a halfpenny into my hat. Jeremiah growled and I said, "Thank you, your grace." But he did not look me in the eye. I think he had higher things on his mind, as priests usually do. They are wilfully blind. Their God is their bellies; they are devouring wolves in sheep's clothing.'

Then Elizabeth, with her cat Sultan in her arms, spoke softly to Wedderburn, 'My dear, your father is dead. His crimes have gone to the grave. I remember you quoting your bible: acknowledge no father. I recollect your words: we should think none greater than ourselves. But it's hard without you. And Sultan's missing you too.'

Finally William Davidson, like a ghost, cried in a hoarse voice: 'The Lord Chief Justice asked the God of all mercy and grace to have mercy on my soul. But he had no mercy. I missed you on the scaffold when I most needed a brother. The cold and the sweat and the churning of my belly. I remembered the laughter in the chapel in Hopkins Street and thought how very sweet life is. The rope touched my neck like the caress of a lover and I could feel the hot tears, and the crowd became a blur. What comfort there was in the grace of Jesus!'

Opposite: Emancipation

He began to sing gently to the tune of Redhead:

> *Rock of Ages, cleft for me,*
> *Let me hide myself in Thee;*
> *Let the water and the blood,*
> *From Thy riven side which flowed,*
> *Be of sin the double cure,*
> *Cleanse me from its guilt and power.*
>
> *While I draw this fleeting breath,*
> *When my eyelids close in death,*
> *When I soar to worlds unknown,*
> *See Thee on Thy judgement-throne:*
> *Rock of Ages, cleft for me,*
> *Let me hide myself in Thee.*

As Davidson finished singing the hymn, Wedderburn sat up, complaining, 'Who's singing that Methodist hymn. I'm not dead, you know! I'm only in this dank, dark dungeon in Dorchester. In fact I've written another letter to the Archbishop of Canterbury.'

He took out a paper from his pocket, but his assembled audience cried out 'no reading'. Wedderburn smiled and recited the letter by heart: 'A critical, historical and admonitory letter to the Right Reverend Father in God, His Grace the Lord Archbishop of Canterbury.' At the mention of his name the clockwork Archbishop started whirring and clicking, his arm moving up and down blessing the congregation. Wedderburn continued:

This is also addressed to all Catholics, Antinomians, Unitarians, Calvinists, Arminians, Swedenborgians, Quakers, Southcottians, Muggletonians, Sandemanians, Jumpers, Dunkers and Mumpers.

After mature deliberation, I have come to a decision, that the most strenuous efforts that can be made on the part of the clergy will now be totally ineffectual to dislodge the Deists from their strongholds, and consequently that instant recourse must be had to the arm of the law, but not in the negligent and slovenly manner in which it has lately been done.

I do now take upon me humbly to recommend the following measures:

A bill to be brought into parliament to decree the punishment of death, by burning, to every author who shall write, every speaker who shall discourse, every printer who shall print, and every bookseller who shall publish the most trifling work against our holy religion, or the church or clergy, as established by law.

That all magistrates shall be ordered and empowered to enter and search every house throughout the empire for blasphemous publications, and cause the same to be publicly burnt in the centre of every town, village and parish; and at the same time compelling every person in whose possession any such works are found, to appear before an open tribunal, and swear never to promulgate the sentiments they have imbibed from such deistical, sceptical, or atheistical and blasphemous books.

And that the said act may be more effectually carried into execution, I here subjoin the names of those books which I could wish in the first place to be proscribed. I do not pretend that the list contains every sceptical book which ought to be burnt, as I have only mentioned such as have come under my own observation, and occur to my memory at this moment, trusting that some zealous Christian will supply whatever may be deficient in my humble efforts.

Hobbes's 'Leviathan', Locke's 'Essay on Human Understanding', Hume's 'Essays', Voltaire's 'Philosophical Dictionary', Rousseau's 'Emile', Diderot's 'Thoughts on Religion', Paine's deistical 'Age of Reason', Shelley's atheistical 'Queen Mab', Tommy Spence's radical songs and Allen Davenport's revolutionary poems.

I am, with the greatest veneration, Reverend Father, your devoted servant in Christ, Robert Wedderburn.

> *Of all the tyrannies which curse mankind,*
> *Those are the worst, which persecute the mind.*

Davenport led the applause and cheering. He pointed at the shuffling clockwork figures and performed his poem with vigour:

> *Ah! Why, while the rich tables of the great*
> *Groan with the weight of gold and silver plate,*
> *And sumptuous viands cull'd from every part,*
> *And choicest wines to cheer and glad the heart!*
> *Why, while their wardrobes boast a splendid store*
> *Of rich apparel, brought from every shore,*
> *And while their chests contain exhaustless bags,*
> *Do millions pine through want, in filth and rags!*
> *Whence this unequal state with ills so fraught;*
> *Ah, when and where was such a system taught?*

Is this refinement? This a civil state?
Is this requir'd to make a nation great?
Then greatness is the peasant's greatest foe,
For he was happier when things were not so.
In other times, e'en to the meanest clown,
The hateful name of pauper was unknown;
But now the poor stand on the beggar's side,
The scoff and scorn of opulence and pride!

Wedderburn followed Davenport's direction and began examining the clockwork figures. He spoke pensively, with a wry smile on his face:

Situated as I am, in solitary confinement, I have had much time for thought and the idea has come to me of inventing a clockwork parson, an automaton which could even imitate the human voice. If it were successful, the clergy could be totally annihilated, suppressed and abolished. Every parish could then purchase one of these clockwork parsons and retain the person who officiates as clerk, to superintend, keep clean and wind up the mechanical parson.

The advantages of the proposed plan are many. Our holy religion could no longer be brought into disgrace by the bad lives of the clergy, for the clockwork parson could not be guilty of adultery, fornication, drunkenness or gambling.

Can parishioners derive the benefit they ought from the holy Gospel of God, when preached by a man who they have reason to abhor, who they may perhaps consider as a hypocrite, a knave and an overbearing tyrant? Can they consider such a man a fit herald to proclaim the doctrine of the meek and lowly Jesus, or a proper successor to the humble fishermen, his disciples? And is not this a most important consideration at a period when we can hardly keep our heads above water, and are threatened every moment either with bankruptcy or revolution?

It may be said that my plan deprives the government of considerable support by destroying the legitimate clergy who have ever been convenient tools in their hands wherewith to keep the bulk of the people in subjection, by preaching up non-resistance, passive obedience, the divine right of kings, or any other doctrine which might suit their purpose. But I propose to give the neighbouring magistrates the superintendence of the sermons which are to be spoken by the automaton. Consequently he will become a more certain and uniform engine of the government than the live parson.

Slaves celebrating freedom

There have been instances of stubborn, headstrong and independent men getting into the church and what has happened once may happen again. Therefore, as the times are getting worse, and arbitrary measures more necessary to keep the 'swinish multitude' in order, care must be taken against such an occurrence, by adopting my clockwork parson, who will at the end of every discourse say, 'Fear God, honour the King, pay your Taxes, be humble and quiet that you may enter the kingdom of Heaven'.

At this point, the clockwork figures clanked into life again, repeating the mantra in unison several times. Then the mechanical voices gradually faded as Wedderburn resumed:

I shall be told that it is very inhuman to turn 20,000 clergymen thus suddenly out of employ, but of what weight is humanity in the scale, when the good of the state depends on it? Will not the retrenching of £3,000,000 annually paid to the clergy enable us better to pay the government taxes? How many thousands of labourers and artisans have been starved in consequence of the introduction of machinery and dispensing with human labour; but are a few thousand souls to be thought of, when by this means the great capitalist has been able to sell his goods cheap and pay the king's taxes, which he could not otherwise have done?

I am no enemy of religion, or the church, or the government, but a friend to the whole – staunch and loyal to the back-bone. This is no wicked, ironical, sarcastic, Jesuitical libel, aimed at the destruction of the church, as by law established, but merely the suggestion of a slight improvement in one of the wheels of the great state machine, for the benefit of the whole. In an awful hour like the present, when Jacobinism and infidelity are making such rapid strides, it is the duty of every good man to exert those talents which divine providence has given him, in suggesting any idea that may possibly save us from the dreadful gulf of ruin which stares us in the face.

If this proposal for clockwork parsons proves successful, then why not extend it to kings and lords, judges and lawyers, landlords and members of parliament, fathers and slave-holders. The possibilities are endless. Come on, my Jon Kanoo.

As he pointed to each clockwork figure in turn, they whirred and creaked, but finally jammed stuck in awkward poses. Billy Waters struck up a song and all the human beings joined in triumphantly:

> *They who fell in fields of glory,*
> *They who died to make us free,*
> *They who live in deathless story,*
> *Point the way to victory.*

Midst the fight shall they attend us,
 Who for freedom fought and fell,
Hovering near, from harm defend us,
 Guarded by a sacred spell.

They who burst the chain enslaving,
 They who curb'd the tyrant's power
They who died their people saving,
 Guard us now in battle's hour.

Tyrants tremble! Freedom calls us,
 Justice lifts the awful scale,
The tyrant's frown no more appals us,
 Justice – freedom – must prevail.

As the last verse rose to a crescendo, lightning flashed through the air and struck the clockwork figures. Sparks flew as their limbs thrashed about in all directions. Their legs buckled and, at the ensuing claps of thunder, they all collapsed in a jagged heap on the ground.